People and plac

HIGH WEALD

The Church of St Peter and St Paul, Wadhurst

Brigid Chapman
Illustrations by Helen Fenton

By the same author
The Weathervanes of Sussex
East Sussex Inns
West Sussex Inns
Royal Visitors to Sussex
Night of the Fires
A Surrey Quiz Book
Brighton in the Fifties

First published in 1999 by S. B. Publications,
c/o 19 Grove Road, Seaford, East Sussex BN25 1TP

ISBN 1 85770 153 4

Designed and typeset by CGB, Lewes
Printed by Island Press
3 Cradle Hill Industrial Estate, Seaford, East Sussex BN25 3JE
Tel: 01323 490222

CONTENTS

ACKNOWLEDGEMENTS

WITHOUT the wonderful co-operation of everyone I have badgered by telephone and tormented with questions this story of the people and places of the East Sussex High Weald could not have been told. I am deeply grateful to:

Beryl Bradley, local history librarian at Crowborough branch of the East Sussex County Library; Pauline Braban, clerk to Burwash Parish Council; Valerie Collings for information on and picture of St Joseph's church, Burwash; Simon Forman of estate agents Freeman Forman, Heathfield; Peter Gillies, Windmill Press, Hadlow Down; Dr J Goulton, clerk to Wadhurst Parish Council; C W Hepworth, clerk to Buxted Parish Council; Ann Jenner, president of Hurst Green Local History Society; P C Keeley, clerk to Dallington Parish Council; Barbara Laird, Mayfield; Nigel Marshall, East Sussex County Council Landscape Group; David Martin, Rape of Hastings Archeological Survey; Judy Moore, JEM Editorial Services, Lewes; Peter Newnham, Cross in Hand; Gerry Sherwin, assistant AONB officer, High Weald Unit; and Kenneth Thomas, clerk to Etchingham Parish Council.

Cover photograph by Martin Jones, supplied by the High Weald Unit.

THE HIGH WEALD AREA OF OUTSTANDING NATURAL BEAUTY

The High Weald extends from Horsham in West Sussex east to Tenterden in Kent. Its northern edge is above Tunbridge Wells and its southern extremity is at Hastings. From there it slants back at a 45° angle to Heathfield, Haywards Heath and Horsham. The High Weald is a nationally important landscape. It was designated an Area of Outstanding Natural Beauty in 1983 in order to aid the protection and management of some of the most beautiful but vulnerable areas of working countryside.

THE EAST SUSSEX HIGH WEALD

Location: That part of the High Weald between the A26 Uckfield to Tunbridge Wells road and the A21 Robertsbridge to Tonbridge Road. The B2100 runs along the northern ridge, the A267 along the central ridge and the A265 along the southern one.

DINOSAURS have left their footprints, noble families their manor houses, the early church its abbeys, smugglers their legends, and a great iron industry its artefacts on the three forest ridges and the valleys between them that form the High Weald of East Sussex.

It is high and it is healthy, and everywhere the views are magnificent. Great writers have made their homes here – Kipling at Burwash, Sir Arthur Conan Doyle, the creator of Sherlock Holmes, at Crowborough – and every community has had its characters. In tenth century Mayfield St Dunstan dealt with the devil; a couple of hundred years later an Abbot of Robertsbridge was sent to Germany to sort out King Richard l's ransom; 'Mad Jack' Fuller, squire of Brightling, built a tower to win a bet; the 3rd Earl of Liverpool moved a village and its inhabitants out of Buxted Park. . .

Until well into historical times dense forest covered the Weald – from the Old English *wald*, which means a forest. It was used by the Saxon and Norman farmers who lived on its fringes as seasonal pasture for their pigs, and the network of narrow, winding roads in the region is, to an extent, based on the tracks along which the swineherds would drive the animals in their care. From pannage to pasture was a logical step and soon the woodland was being cleared to provide land for stock – the soil was of too poor a quality for cereal crops – and later to feed the furnaces of the iron industry.

Small self-sufficient communities grew up in these clearings, their isolation forced upon them by the lack of a road link with anywhere but the settlements on the forest fringes from whence they came. As more people moved into the area and more trees were cleared clusters of cottages grew up around the previously isolated churches and the old Wealden villages of Mayfield and Buxted, Burwash, Wadhurst, Old Heathfield and Robertsbridge, Etchingham and Dallington came into being.

There had been an iron industry of a sort in the Weald from the time of the Roman occupation for the raw material was easily obtained from nodules close to the surface in beds of Wadhurst clay. It would be carted off to furnaces set up beside a river or stream, for water was needed to cool the molten metal. A bed of clay, about a foot thick and with a diameter of about twelve feet, formed the base of the furnace. It was covered with loose sand on which thick blocks of sandstone were packed together and topped with another layer of sand. On top of this came a thick layer a broken charcoal mixed with limestone and then a layer of broken ironstone.

The layers of charcoal and ore were repeated five or six times in circles of lessening diameter and a cone of clay, about six inches (150mm) thick and about 6ft (2m) high, was plastered round them with a vent at the top and six or so holes round the base to take the nozzles of the goatskin bellows that were operated by hand or by foot to keep the fire at a constant heat. It was not a particularly efficient form of smelting as much iron was left in the ore but the metal that did emerge could be fashioned at once into tools or weapons without further processing. When the furnace had cooled it was knocked down and the residue of slag, charcoal and scorched clay spread out and a new hearth built on top of it.

In the fifteenth century two innovations from the Continent, the water-powered bloomery forge and the blast furnace, turned a little local industry into a big business. It became even bigger when the use of gunpowder created the need for cannon and, after the first one had been cast successfully in iron – earlier models were made of iron bars held together with strong hoops like a barrel – there were lucrative government contracts to be filled.

The subsistence farmers of the High Weald became smiths – and rich –

Huggetts Furnace mill where, in 1543, if tradition is correct:
Master Hogge and his man John,
They did cast the first cannon

almost overnight. They mined the ironstone, crushed it with giant hammers, fired it in their furnaces and, because they were still farmers at heart, called ingots of iron weighing more than 1,000lbs (500kg) 'sows' and those weighing less 'pigs'. They produced cartwheel rims, ploughshares, agricultural implements, locks, keys and candle brackets as well as cannon. The iron founders of Sussex were also the only ones to make iron firebacks and iron grave slabs, of which there are more than thirty in Wadhurst parish church alone.

The iron industry also changed the scenery and affected the pattern of village life. So much timber was cut down to fuel the furnaces that there were fears that not enough would be left to build ships. From being thickly forested whole areas were stripped of almost all growing things and scarred with deep pits from which the ironstone was mined. Artificial ponds were created to get a head of water to power furnace or forge and streams and rivulets were dammed.

Where there was ironstone there was work for all, not only in the forests and at the foundries but in getting the finished products to the consumers, for it took a lot of men a lot of time to get loads of cannon and bar iron along tracks of mud to navigable rivers and to the coast. The local economy flourished as both labourer and landowner had money in hand. The former settled his family in a timber framed cottage, the latter built handsome houses like Bateman's at Burwash – an under-taking which gave even more employment to the artisans – and embarked on good works.

When the iron industry collapsed at the end of the eighteenth century with the discovery of coal near the iron deposits in the Midlands, the farmer/smiths went back to agriculture, this time growing hops and planting orchards as well as raising cattle, sheep and pigs. There was a terrible period of transition. Farmers were beginning to replace men with machines and angry mobs of labourers, often accompanied by women and children, stormed around the countryside reinforcing their demands for a living wage by acts of vandalism and threats to the lives of individual employers.

The Poor Law Reform Act of 1834, which relieved parishes of sole responsibility for their own paupers, and a revival of the national economy in the reign of Victoria, brought the railways and some new wealth to the Weald both in terms of cash and culture. Well-to-do families from London moved in, attracted by the fresh air of the forest ridges and the splendour of the scenery which had by then recovered from the onslaught of the iron industry.

The newcomers built schools and churches wherever there was a need for them and few existing edifices escaped the almost too thorough schemes of the restoration they were only too happy to finance. Like those who came before them, be they Normans invaders, French marauders, Flemish weavers or Spanish gunsmiths, they enriched the High Weald and were absorbed by it. They even, through the turnpike trusts, managed to do something about the awful roads, although as late as the 1890s the de Muriettas of Wadhurst Park were in the habit of sending a waggon drawn by a team of oxen to the station. In wet weather it was the only way they could be sure a conveyance would be there to meet guests arriving by train.

The turnpikes were a help to the poor as well as the rich. They opened up areas of wasteland on which out-of-work labourers built shacks for their families and later, with their traditional squatters' rights established, more permanent homes. Among the hamlets, each with its alehouse and its chapel, that began in this way are Broad Oak, Burwash Common and Burwash Weald along the Hurst Green turnpike and Punnett's Town and Three Cups on the road to Battle.

The twentieth century brought even greater improvements in communications. The motor car and main line train services to London opened up the area to those who wished to live in the country but had to work in the capital. Places with stations, like Buxted, Crowborough, Etchingham and Robertsbridge, grew in population and prosperity for the newcomers needed shops and services, schools for their children and something to do in their leisure time. Fortunately the influx was fairly gradual and communities could expand at their own pace. Unlike the coastal strip, where builders responded to excessive demand by running up the rows of terraced houses and estates of bungalows, the towns and villages of the forest ridges have kept their character and their countryside.

There are no over-precincted mini-Croydons in the High Weald of East Sussex. Burwash's High Street retains its medieval magnificence, Mayfield its ecclesiastical elegance, Robertsbridge its old timbered buildings. Even such late developers as Crowborough and modern Heathfield have a friendly fresh air bustle about them – and a whole lot of history and some splendid views on their doorsteps.

BRIGHTLING

The temple Smirke built in Brightling Park and, left, the round tower in the wood on the road to Oxley's Green.

WHERE TO FIND THE FOLLIES

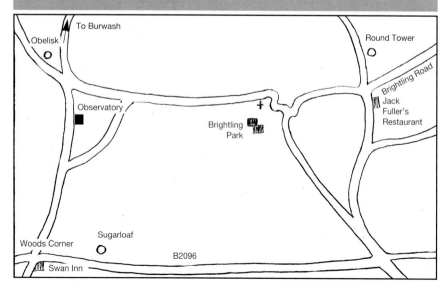

BRIGHTLING

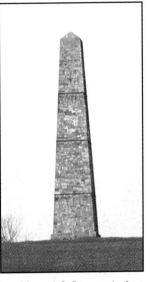

Location: Off the B2096 on the southern forest ridge, two and a half miles south of Burwash.
Population: 403.
Station: Robertsbridge.

THE existence of this small village is announced from afar by an obelisk on the highest point in the area – the 646ft high Brightling Down. Brightling Needle, as it came to be called because of its resemblance to Cleopatra's Needle on the Embankment, is on the site of the chain of beacons that was fired across Sussex when the Armada was sighted in the Channel. It was 'misfired' in 1586, when fifty ships were reported sailing towards Brighton 'as though they had purpose to come to the shore.' The 1808 edition of Holinshed's *Chronicles* records the incident:

> 'Beacons were none fired (although the contrary was reported) but one at Burrish (as was said) from which error some perhaps might in like sort be fired in Kent, but yet verie few.'

The 'invaders' turned out to Dutchmen bound for Holland laden with merchandise from Spain. They were ten of them, not fifty, and they were 'friends and no enemies' who had been forced to hug the coast because of the easterly wind. The Spanish Armada turned up two years later.

The obelisk on the beacon site is just one of a number of strangely shaped structures John Fuller had built in the locality in the early 1800s. As a twenty year old in 1777 he had inherited the family fortune and Rose Hill – as Brightling Park was then called – but did not waste his wealth on riotous living. Instead he served as MP for Sussex from 1801 to 1812, founded two Fellowships at the Royal Institution, commissioned the artist J M W Turner to paint a number of Sussex landscapes and bought Bodiam Castle to save it from total destruction.

Fuller was known variously known as 'Mad Jack' 'Hippopotamus', or 'Honest Jack' Fuller – the first because of his follies, both in and out of

THE NAMES ON THE NEEDLE

Brightling Needle, which resembles the Wellington monument in Phoenix Park, Dublin, and was possibly erected for the same reason – to commemorate the Iron Duke's victory at Waterloo – was designed by Robert Smirke, an architect responsible for many of Fuller's 'jobs for the boys' projects. All that is inscribed on the obelisk are the names of the father and son who did some repairs to the concrete cap:

R Croft 1889 and Charles Croft, July 29 1889, aged 16 years.

✳ ✳ ✳

the House of Commons from which he was once escorted by the Sergeant at Arms for insulting the Speaker (he called him 'an insignificant little chap'); the second because in later life he weighed twenty-two stone; and the third because of his refusal of the peerage he was offered by Pitt, with the words: 'I was born Jack Fuller and Jack Fuller I'll die'.

Much of the fortune he inherited was founded on the slave trade, for it was brought into the family when an earlier John Fuller married Elizabeth, daughter of Fulke Rose, a rich plantation owner in Jamaica. 'Mad Jack' saw nothing odd in arguing furiously against the emancipation of slaves whenever the matter was raised in the House and at the same time spending considerable sums on providing work for the people in his parish.

His earliest architectural excesses were at Rose Hill. He started in 1803 with a small summerhouse built entirely of Coadeware artificial stone. Two years later he commissioned Robert Smirke to build him a classic temple as a focal point at the southern end of the park. The result was a single circular room (pictured on page ten) surrounded by a Doric colonnade and topped by a small dome surrounded by a decorated frieze.

Smirke's next assignment was an observatory, for astronomy was a fashionable interest of the gentry in those days, inspired by Sir William Herschel's discovery of Uranus. Its telescope dome can be seen from the road to Wood's Corner, outside the four mile long wall around the park which was another of Fuller's labour-intensive construction schemes. For some years after he died the observatory, which is now a private house, was run by a committee as a museum and its camera obscura was a great favourite with to visitors.

The last of Smirke's buildings is the clumsy pyramid-shaped stone structure 'Mad Jack' had built in Brightling churchyard during his lifetime to serve as his tomb. According to local tradition he was buried sitting upright in an iron chair at a table on which there was placed a jug of claret and some glasses. Broken glass was scattered on the ground outside to cut the devil's cloven hooves, should he appear.

Squire Fuller was, in fact, buried beneath the tomb in the orthodox way and there was no broken glass scattered around the churchyard, intentionally or otherwise.

On his instructions a marble bust of him by Sir Francis Chantrey was placed in the church of St Thomas à Becket which also contains the barrel organ he gave in 1820 to replace a smaller one which was later sent to a mission in New Zealand and is now in the Wanganiu Museum. As well as the new organ, which has twelve hymns, carols and canticles on each of its two barrels, Fuller gave the men of the choir white smocks, buckskin breeches and yellow stockings to wear for the first service at which it was played. The girls of the choir received red cloaks for the occasion.

Fuller's first genuine folly – built for no practical purpose but to win a bet – is the Sugarloaf, which is on the left hand side of the B2096 Woods

* * *

ANYONE
AT HOME?

In the 1930s, so it is said in the locality, a Mr Lulham lived in the small room inside the Sugarloaf and raised a family there.

* * *

Corner to Netherfield road. This 20ft high whitish coloured stone cone, which looks as sugar did when delivered in bulk to grocers and confectioners, was run up almost overnight so Fuller could claim he could see Dallington church spire from Rose Hill.

Another folly is the 30ft high round tower in the woods on the right hand side of the road from Brightling parish church to Oxley's Green. From it, so it was said, Fuller checked the progress of the restoration work at Bodiam Castle – which was, no doubt, why he had it built. Its door is always open and anyone with a head for heights can climb the iron stairway and see the full splendour of the Wealden landscape from the upper windows.

Brightling no longer has a village inn. Gone is the Green Man opposite the church, where in the eighteenth century the landlady 'baked light cakes in the forenoon and puddings in the evening for sale', on July 7, the feast day of St Thomas à Becket. The innkeeper offended Jack Fuller in some way so he ordered his removal, inn and all.

In 1834, the year Fuller died, the innkeeper opened a new Green Man outside the parish at Oxley's Green. A later licensee, obviously unaware of past feuds, changed its name to the Fuller's Arms. Today it is Jack Fuller's Restaurant.

A hidden industry

GONE too is Brightling furnace from which the iron founding members of the Fuller family made their money. But the gypsum mine in Ashen Wood is still in production and ore from it is now carried overland on the only horizontally-curved conveyor in Europe, to be processed at British Gypsum's works at

Mountfield into the plaster which is used to make plasterboard.

When the Sub Wealden Committee was set up in 1872 'to ascertain by the experiment of boring the actual nature and thickness' of the geological strata beneath the Weald, it was 'purely for scientific purposes', the public was told, 'not to discover coal or other minerals'. Work started in Limekiln Wood in the parish of Netherfield and in 1873 a 50ft deep bed of gypsum was found about 250ft below the surface.

From the end of the nineteenth century the mineral mined from the Wealden rock was conveyed by an aerial ropeway through the woods to the factory and processing plant at Mountfield. There most of it was turned into the wall plaster, Sirapite, and bagged up to go to various parts of the country. Plaster of Paris was also produced from the gypsum and some of the mined raw stone was used to repair the roads.

The continuous overland conveyor that replaced the aerial ropeway in the 1980s cost £7 million and took eighteen months to construct. It is 4.7km

Mining gypsum at Brightling in the 1930s with pick, shovel and wheelbarrow.

***

GYPSUM IN THE COAL HOLE

The discovery of gypsum was marked by a local rhymster, obviously unimpressed by the 'no hunt for coal' propaganda, with this somewhat halting verse:

They digged a hole to find the coal
But they found 'twas gypsum and salt;
So on they went with same intent
Till they broke the tool and called halt.

***

long, consists of a steel cord with moulded rubber covers, and can carry 450 tonnes of gypsum an hour from the Brightling mine to the Mountfield works.

There is little visible indication that a thriving industry and large employer of local labour has been in continuous operation in the woods of this part of the Weald for more than a century. Apart from occasional signs bearing the name British Gypsum Ltd beside concrete roads that lead off into the trees the only indication of activity are the white clouds of steam that now and then appear on the skyline. Seen in the sunlight, from the garden of the Bear Hotel or other vantage points on the south side of Burwash High Street, these steam clouds look just like any other bit of fair weather cumulus until they disappear as suddenly as they have appeared.

A Victorian weekender

JACK FULLER was not the only Member of Parliament with property in the New World and in the parish of Brightling. William Smith, who owned the 100 acre Scalands estate between Brightling and Robertsbridge, represented the Tory interests in Norwich from 1790 to 1825 and had land in Savannah. However, unlike Fuller he was totally opposed to slavery and refused compensation for the loss of his American estates after the Declaration of Independence.

His son, Benjamin, held even more radical views, particularly on education which he believed should be enlightened, non-sectarian and progressive. He was equally unorthodox about his domestic arrangements, fathering five children on Miss Leigh,

16

a milliner of Hastings, and failing to marry her. But he was no misogynist and settled £300 a year on his daughter, Barbara, when she came of age in 1848 and gave her the freehold of the Westminster Infants' School in Vincent Square SW1.

Encouraged by her cousin, Florence Nightingale, Barbara Leigh-Smith became one of the first feminist activists and campaigned to change the law under which a married woman had no rights to her own property, not even to her watch or her wallet. However, to begin with the school took up most of her time. She ran it as a truly mixed infants – boys and girls of any or no religious persuasion, the children of the leisured and the labouring classes. Parents who could afford to paid sixpence (2fip) a week, for others it was free. It was hard and exacting work and Barbara and her helpers often felt the need to get away from it all. Which is how she came to build what was probably the first weekend cottage in East Sussex.

Scalands was on the road from Brightling to Robertsbridge, where there was a new station with trains to London. The house, built of hand-made bricks and timber grown on her father's estate, had a front door leading directly into the living room. On the sides of its open fireplace her friends – among them Marian Evans, better known to the reading public as George Eliot, garden designer Gertrude Jekyll and pre-Raphaelite painter Dante Gabriel Rossetti – all signed their names.

The house was considerably extended by her husband, Eugene Bodichon, a French surgeon she met in Algiers in 1857 and married a few months later. They toured the west coast of North America from Quebec to the Gulf of Mexico on their honeymoon and brought back to Brightling seeds of a tulip tree and a Californian redwood which are now each more than 100ft in height.

Barbara died in 1891 and is buried, as is her father, in Brightling churchyard. Scalands House was severely damaged by fire in 1950 and was virtually derelict, its Jekyll-designed garden totally overgrown, when it was bought in the 1980s by a Fellow of the Chartered Society of Designers and has since been sympathetically restored.

BRIGHTLING

Haunted house is 'fired'

* * *

A TWICE TOLD
TALE

*It appears there was
more than one published
account of the
Brightling haunting.
'I remember to have
seen the same formerly
in a book lent by Mrs
Dear of Burwash to
Mrs Burgess' notes
William Hayley in the
margin of his
manuscript.
In another note, dated
October 27 1786, he
refers to seeing 'a larger
account at Mr Katt's
at Robertsbridge
Abbey.'*

* * *

A FIRE of a much stranger sort destroyed Hodges Mill farmhouse at Brightling in 1659. An account of the bizarre incidents that preceded its destruction is among the historical material relating to East Sussex collected by the Reverend William Hayley and left by him to the British Museum.

The tale is told in a book published in 1662 entitled *A Mirror or Looking Glass for Saints and Sinners,* in a chapter headed 'A Strange Judgement in Sussex.' The material was supplied, according to Samuel Clarke, the editor and publisher, by the Reverend Joseph Bennett, who was ejected from the living of Brightling in that year for nonconformity. It starts, in classic ghost story fashion, with an awful warning.

'At or near the house of Joseph Cruttenden of Brightling' a servant girl was told by an old woman that 'sad calamities were coming on her Master and Dame, their house shall be fired and many troubles befall them'. If the girl repeated what she had been told 'the devil would tear her to pieces'. If she kept quiet she would not be hurt.

On the night of November 9 dirt and dust were thrown at her master and mistress while they were in bed. When they got up and knelt to pray the disturbance ceased. The same thing happened at noon next day and before night fell one end of their house caught fire and, although it was burnt to the ground 'it flamed not'. The story goes on:

> 'They rake it down; it flashes somewhat like gunpowder; as they stopped it there it began in another place and then in another until the whole house burnt down. Some say something like a Black Bull was seen tumbling about.'

The couple spent the rest of the night collecting their belongings together and next day Colonel John Busbridge of Haremere Hall let them move to another of his houses in the parish. No sooner were their possessions inside than the disturbances started up again:

'Ye house fireth, endeavours are made to quench it but in vain till ye goods are thrown out, when it ceased with little or no help'.

The couple, homeless for a second time, took shelter in a hut and a curious crowd gathered outside. The arrival of the Reverend Joseph Bennett started a barrage of brickbats. He was hit by a knife and a bowl was thrown at his back but the moment he started to pray the manifestations ceased. When hit by a horseshoe 'which flew to the man and strike him and arise again of its own accord, fly to the man and strike him in the midst of a hundred people' the husband confessed to being a thief and taking goods on the Sabbath Day.

Not until November 15, when Mr Bennett arranged with three neighbouring ministers, Mr Golden, Mr Weller and Mr Bradshaw, to hold a fast day and each to preach a sermon, did the disturbances stop.

Subsequently the servant girl told her mistress of the warning and the matter was taken sufficiently seriously for two magistrates, Captain Collins of Socknersh and Colonel Busbridge, to send for an old woman previously suspected of witchcraft. She was 'watched and searched for twenty-four hours' but finally released because the girl could not make a positive identification.

BURWASH

The village sign was made by Jim Smith in 1973 and stands on the only piece of common land in village – a square yard of the front garden of Pope's Cottage in the High Street, which was given to the parish by estate agents Brian and Linda Mathews.
On the three shields above the sign are the arms of the de Burghersh and Pelham families and the county arms.

✳ ✳ ✳

BURWASH, known locally as Bur'rish, never made the *Domesday Book* under any of its aliases – Burgerrsh, Burghese, Burghesshe, Borgaessch, Borgerse, Borwhesse and Borwarssh. Perhaps the compilers of this 1086 census of population and resources could not find anything they considered worthy of record in what was then a heavily wooded and agriculturally unproductive area.

The Normans reversed the old Saxon system by which an Englishman held land as of right, chose his alderman, and it was they who elected the king. Under the feudal system the Crown owned all the land and it was parcelled out to the king's family and friends in return for allegiance, a supply of men for military service, and the payment of taxes and tribute. Sussex was divided into rapes – the only county in the country to be so apportioned – and a manor consisted of a thousand acre plot within a rape, held in return for at least knight service.

The manors of Burwash and Burghest were in the Rape of Hastings which Robert, Count of Eu, held from the king. He was one of William of Normandy's best generals and had supplied thirty of the ships that brought the invasion force of 9,000 troops across the Channel in 1066. In return he and his heirs received quite a large section of Sussex. They lost it in 1244 when the then Count of Eu decided to offer allegiance to Louis IX of France rather than to Henry III of England, who gave the forfeited lands to his seven year old son, Edward.

The manor of Burwash was administered for the Crown by Bernard de Savoy, the king's half brother, and in 1247 he was ordered, as keeper of the park at Burwash, to provide four deer from it to 'for use of the king's children at Windsor'. He was also ordered to 'make a mill at the Manor of Burwash' for which the king would pay.

An inquisition of 1280, which reads rather like a tax return, shows that income from the manor in that year was a princely £18 12s 2d. However, by 1344 when it was held by the first Earl of Richmond, the income from it had dropped to £9 9s 6d.

The manor of Burgherst was held by a family of that name in the fourteenth century. A Henry Burghersh was made Bishop of Lincoln by Edward II, lost the king's favour and the bishopric, and was later reinstated. He expressed his gratitude to the king by helping Queen Isabella depose him. Thomas Fuller has little to say to the credit of this Bishop Burghersh in his *Worthies*. The entry reads:

> 'He was one of Noble Alliance. And when that is said, all is said to his commendation, being otherwise neither good for Church nor State, Sovereign nor Subjects. Covetous, Ambitious, Rebellious, Injurious. . . He was twice Lord Treasurer, once Lord Chancellor and was sent over as Ambassador to the Duke of Bavaria. He died *Anno Domini* 1340.'

But when Henry Burghersh died his spirit did not rest. Because of his habit of annexing other men's lands into his park he was condemned to haunt the scenes of his crimes as a green ghost of a forester.

A number of illustrious families held the Rape of Hastings and its manors until the end of manorial rights in 1925. Among them were the Pelhams who had the lordship for three and half centuries and the Earls of Westmoreland, whose eldest sons have the courtesy title of Baron Burghese. The last Lady of the Manor of Burwash was the Countess of Ashburnham.

Common, Weald and Town

THERE are three Burwashes on the A265 which runs along the 300ft high forest ridge separating the valleys of the Rother and the Dudwell – Burwash Common, Burwash Weald and Burwash Town.

It was on the Common, in the summer of 1747, that guns made to a special pattern for Ireland at John Fuller's Brightling furnace were damaged on their way to Woolwich. 'A little ornamental ball, no bigger than a tennis ball, at the end of each gun was knocked off six of them but so artfully put on again with a screw that I hope there will be no occasion of making use of the enclosed advertisement', wrote John Fuller to the Duke of Newcastle, who had ordered the guns. The advertisement he enclosed offered a reward of ten guineas for information leading to the conviction of the 'evil, despised, malicious people' who did the damage.

In the early 1800s the Common and its neighbouring hamlet, Burwash Weald, were places to be avoided by the respectable. No one cared to risk riding across Burwash Down after nightfall and isolated householders lived in fear of attacks by burglars. A later Burwash Common resident, Charles Trower, writing in the *Sussex Archeological Collections* of 1869, described the area at the turn of the century as 'the birthplace or sheltering place of rick burners, sheep stealers and thieves' who 'gained an illicit profit, and led dissolute lives, in conveying kegs of brandy up the country with relays of horses from the sea coast'.

There was not much else they could do, apart from poaching in which they also indulged, to feed themselves and their families at that time. The parish did its best to find jobs for the jobless. It rented Bough Farm on the edge of the Common and put eighty men to work on its 96 acres, not with ploughs but in a labour intensive form of spade husbandry. On one occasion, to relieve the boredom of the back-breaking work of digging all day, the men at Bough Farm solemnly staged a ceremonial funeral for a dead robin. It cost the parish £20 in lost time.

Good women and good works

THE improvement in the national economy, which began in the mid Victorian era, soon had an effect upon the villages of the High Weald. A number of well-to-do families moved to them from the London area, no doubt attracted by the beautiful scenery, the breathtaking views from the forest ridge and the arrival of the railway in the area.

Burwash Weald's Church of St Philip, pictured below, owes its existence to the three spinster sisters of the Right Reverend Gerald Trower, Bishop of Gibraltar. Georgiana, Emily and Sophia Trower moved from

✳ ✳ ✳

THE COUPLE
IN COURT

*The Sussex Weekly
Advertiser of July 31
carried a full report of
the trial.
Hannah was described
as 'of rather
forbidding aspect
and appeared,
to us at least forty,
although her age is
stated in the calendar
at 32. There was
nothing remarkable
about the male prisoner
(aged 19) but that he
might very well have
passed for her son.'*

✳ ✳ ✳

Redhill to Buckle's Farm in Spring Lane, changed its name to Hollyhurst, and immediately set about good works. They opened a school for the children of the Common and financed the building of the Early English style church, designed by Walter Slater, the architect who was also responsible for the 1856 restoration of St Bartholomew's in Burwash Town.

Today they lie in its churchyard, near the house they lived in, which is now called Buckles. Below the east window of St Philip's there is a marble tablet in memory of the sisters and their generosity. Beneath it there is always a bunch of fresh flowers.

Although Burwash Weald did not have a church within its boundaries it did have an inn. The Wheel, almost exactly opposite Willingford Lane which leads past Forge Farm up Perch Hill to Brightling Needle, had a terrible reputation, not without cause, when it was owned by Frank Russell, a smuggler, receiver of stolen goods and, at eighty three, the father of a two year old child 'of his own begetting'.

'Toy boy' murder case

WHEN Frank's nephew, Benjamin, returned from America in the 1820s and lived at the Wheel with his wife, Hannah, murder was added to the list of crimes with which the inn was associated. While he was away Hannah had started an affair with teenaged Daniel Leney. On his return she lived with both husband and lover and made no secret of her affection for the younger man.

When Benjamin's dead body was found beneath a tree in Gleddish Wood at Brightling where he had gone, it was said, to collect some smuggled goods,

24

the Russell family, who had disapproved of his marriage to Hannah from the outset, immediately suspected the worst and persuaded the parish to finance the prosecution of her and Leney for murder.

The jury at Lewes Assizes heard William Russell, Benjamin's uncle, describe how, accompanied by Hannah and Leney, he moved the body into the woods to make it appear his nephew was collecting smuggled rather than stolen goods. 'My reason for moving it was to hide the shame of the family, in respect to stealing wheat', he said.

At the end of the ten hour hearing Hannah and Leney were convicted of poisoning Benjamin Russell with white arsenic and sentenced to death. Leney was hanged and Hannah was first reprieved on a legal technicality and then pardoned when it was shown that the medical evidence was at fault.

The High Street

THERE has been evolution rather than revolution in the slightly winding half mile of the A265 which is the High Street of Burwash. Many of the timber framed houses, some tile hung, some weatherboarded and screened by a row of pollarded limes on the north side, have been there from medieval times.

The descendants of many of the families who lived in them and traded from them are still in the village today, some just as names on the war memorial, or on the gravestones in the churchyard, others alive and well and active in the community.

Waterhouse Coaches first ran a taxi service from the shed next door to the White Hart and then added coach hire with just the one coach for school outings and to take the cricket and darts teams to matches. The firm, now a flourishing concern based in Eastbourne, was started in 1947 by Derek Waterhouse and his brother, Ted, descendants of the Thomas Waterhouse who is described in the parish records of 1790 as a carrier.

Other members of the Waterhouse family were builders and undertakers. Today, in adjoining High Street premises, the building connection is continued by the Burwash Home Improvements Centre run by Audrey

BURWASH

Houses in the High Street opposite the Bear Hotel

✳ ✳ ✳

FAIR DAYS

THE right to hold a weekly market on Fridays and a fair on the vigil day of St Philip and St James was granted by Henry III in 1252. On or around May 12 every year the fair was held on the field now occupied by the car park.

✳ ✳ ✳

Holman, neé Waterhouse, and C Waterhouse and Sons, funeral directories, now owned by Dorothy Waterhouse.

Until the 1950s the large house now called Cheriton, on the north side of the A265 coming from the west, was the White Hart, the last beer house in Burwash. When licensee Tommy Hook called time there for the last time – it was at 10pm in those days – there was a quantity of beer left so he invited everyone to stay on and drink it for free. This they did and next day there were many sore heads in Burwash and, it is said, a rather put out police sergeant. He thought he had caught a crowd of after-hours drinkers only to learn from the licensee that the pub was officially closed and Tommy was giving the beer away.

In 1971 East Sussex County Council decided to reconstruct the High Street and provide a pavement

26

on the south side – previously without one. There is a plaque on the tile hung frontage next to the shop window of F J Jarvis and Sons, Family Butcher, established 1870 and makers of Burwash Beauty sausages, to 'George H Pierce, foreman with East Sussex County Council, who died on 17 December 1971 whilst in charge of the reconstruction of Burwash High Street.' It ends with the same Latin tag that is on the memorial to Christopher Wren in St Paul's:

Lector si monumentum requies circumspice.

It seems that it was placed there, not because Mr Pierce was accidentally killed or died suddenly while working on the road in front of the house, but because the highways engineer wanted to pay tribute to a long serving member of his department and butcher Jeff Jarvis volunteered the space.

The inn sign of the Rose and Crown, but not the inn itself, is on the corner of the lane that leads to the fire station and to Burwash's first council houses, Coronation Cottages, built in 1936 the year George VI was crowned.

The Rose and Crown, which dates from 1570, is on the west side of the lane, some distance from its sign. Card assemblies were held there on Wednesday evenings in the winter from 1787 and it was the centre of the social life of the area in those days. Well into the last years of the nineteenth century blacksmiths would fire their anvils with loud explosions on November 23 to commemorate their patron saint, St Clement, and repair to the Rose and Crown for a meal of roast pork and sage and onion stuffing. Any breaches of the peace that may have occurred on such festive occasions would be dealt with on the premises for the petty sessions for the district were held at the inn until 1839 when the court moved to the Royal George at Hurst Green.

The magistrates were, in the main, the principal landowners in the locality. Francis Newberry would drive over from Heathfield Park in a

✳ ✳ ✳

WHAT'S IN
A NAME?

*The Admiral Vernon,
on the south side of the
A265 at the eastern end
of the village, is named
after a hero of the War
of Jenkins' Ear.
In this 1739 conflict
with Spain over
trade with South
America, Admiral
Edward Vernon, with
six ships, captured
Portobello, Panama.
London was overjoyed
and peals of bells rang
throughout the city.*

✳ ✳ ✳

coach drawn by four horses; John Fuller would make the shorter journey from Rose Hill at Brightling, also with four horses, while George Courthope from Whiligh and Robert Hawes of Markly were each content with two horse equipages.

The Bell, opposite the church, is another old inn which has in its time varied from raffishness to respectability. It has been a haunt of smugglers, who found a temporary hiding place for their contraband in the tombs in the churchyard across the road, and also welcomed parishioners in need of refreshment after church vestry meetings.

Sussex pub games such a Toad in the Hole and Ringing the Bull can still be played in the bar of the Bell. The first requires players to throw heavy metal discs from a distance of eight feet into a hole in the centre of a lead cushion mounted on a table with a drawer in it. Competitors score two points for every disc that goes in the hole, one point for each one that remains on the cushion and nothing for those that fall to the ground. The object is to score either twenty-one or thirty-one points exactly – you bust if you score twenty-two or thirty-two and must try again for the exact number.

The 'bull' at the Bell is a steer's horn. A metal ring attached to a length of line fixed to the ceiling has to be thrown from a certain distance so it falls onto it – which is not as easy as it sounds although there are some regulars who are on target every time.

The Bear Hotel, built as an inn in the seventeenth century, has expanded considerably since the Kiplings stayed there before moving in to Bateman's. It is now also a motel and has a new garden restaurant at the rear but it has still retained, in the hotel restaurant, the photographs of Rudyard Kipling which adorned the walls of the room in which members of the Kipling Society, founded in 1927, used to meet. Today most of the society's meetings and lectures are in London where it maintains a specialist library at the City University.

Lost – a Wealden hall house

THE fifteenth century Wealden hall house that was Burwash's original rectory was replaced in 1711 by Glebe House, built by a rich rector, the Reverend George Jordan, to the east of the churchyard, from which it is approached by an avenue of oaks. The old rectory was sold by a later incumbent, the Reverend William Curteis, so he could reimburse himself for paying the land tax on it. Over the years the house slid down the social scale to become four tenements, known as Portland Cottages, and in 1968 Battle Rural District Council bought the site for redevelopment. When the old rectory was being stripped for demolition its architectural

Burwash's missing rectory as it would appear if the original framework was re-constructed.

✳ ✳ ✳

WAS THERE A BURGHERSH HOTEL?

Garstons, which stands at right angles to the High Street, behind the church, today presents an unadorned, cream rendered front elevation to the village. When it was built in 1850 it was as an hotel and an illustration in a booklet of that time shows it looking more like a castle than a catering establishment with all its battlements, turrets and Gothic arched windows. How long the Burghersh Hotel lasted, or if indeed it ever actually opened, is not recorded.

✳ ✳ ✳

importance was realised and it was given to the Landmark Trust for re-erection on a site near Crawley. The timbers, all carefully photographed and numbered by members of the Robertsbridge and District Archeological Society, were sent for temporary storage to a barn at Slaugham.

And that is the last anyone has seen of Burwash Rectory. The Landmark Trust has no knowledge of it, neither has East Sussex County Council, Rother District Council nor the Weald and Downland Open Air Museum, which has rebuilt some forty historic buildings rescued from destruction on a 40 acre site at Singleton, and has more in store. Burwash Rectory is not among them.

There was a story current in the late 1970s that Burwash Rectory was going to be re-erected at Cranbrook. David Martin of the Rape of Hastings Architectural Survey vaguely remembers a request from a director of a firm of kitchen equipment suppliers in Tunbridge Wells for photographs of the building that were taken as it was being dismantled. 'There were about 200 of them, and some plans, which were all bought and paid for,' he said.

But the rectory is not in Cranbrook and the Portland Terrace site in the High Street is now occupied by Old Rectory Court, a two storey weatherboarded block of old people's flats.

Close by is Mount House, the centre part of which dates from 1550. The initials B C on a lead cistern on the street frontage probably refer to the Bartholomew or Benjamin Cruttenden who built the house. Later, when the family had, like so many others in the area, made a fortune in the iron industry, it was extended by the addition of a

BURWASH

Chateaubriand, the oldest house in Burwash, has the remains of a unique quasi-aisle dating from the thirteenth century.

gabled east wing. However, it was still quite a modest home when Obedience Cruttenden was born there in 1587. Her arrival brought a lasting benefit to the poor of Burwash for she was such a good wife to Thomas Nevitt, the rich London merchant she married, that he set up a charitable trust with the Girdlers' Company to produce an annual payment to the needy at Christmas.

When Obedience died at the early age of thirty-two the grieving widower set up two memorials to her, one a tablet in the parish church and another a `stately monument' in St Benedict's churchyard, Paul's Wharf, London.The verses on her memorial in the church credit Obedience Cruttenden with a variety of virtues:

> Ne'er Nature framed a better wife.
> By laws divine she squared her life,
> She was not proud, nor high in aught,
> Save when to Heav'n she advanced her thought. . .

Next to Mount House is Rampyndene, the largest and most opulent in appearance of all the gentlemen's residences in the High Street. It was

The south side of the High Street showing Rampyndene and St Bartholomew's church.

* * *

GONE AWAY

In spite of the efforts he made to secure his wife's entry into Heaven, Captain Feilden left her body behind when he moved to the West Country. The next occupant of Rampyndene – his brother, Arctic explorer Colonel Henry Wemyss Feilden – had the remains removed and buried in the churchyard.

* * *

built in 1699 by John Butler, who made his money out of timber rather than iron founding, and had his initials set in a panel above the door.

A later occupant set the village tongues wagging. When Captain John Leyland Feilden's wife died in 1887 the rector, with whom he had had a doctrinal disagreement, was not informed. Instead Captain Feilden had the body embalmed and placed in a crate which he kept in an outbuilding to await the Second Coming. It was then to be shipped at once to Palestine for burial. He had the unnerving habit of asking visitors to Rampyndene if they would like to see his wife. Those unaware of the situation would politely say `yes' and were taken to the outhouse to be introduced to the corpse.

Socknersh Manor, which lies about one and a quarter miles south of the A275 to Etchingham, has even more gruesome associations. The porches above the front and back entrances are supported by grotesque corbels known traditionally as the 'baby killers' because one of them appears to be holding a headless infant. It has been suggested that this figure closely resembles Sir Thomas Lunsford, a Cavalier colonel accused by the Roundheads, quite wrongfully, of cannibalism. Several rhymes of the time spread the seventeenth century equivalent of political sleaze in verse. One runs:

> From Fielding and from Vavasour
> Both ill-affected men
> From Lunsford eke deliver use
> Who eateth up children!'

A ballad about the Battle of Edgehill, after which he was taken prisoner, continues the canard:

> The Post that came from Banbury
> Riding in his blue rocket
> He swore he saw when Lundsford fell
> A child's arm in his pocket

The baby killer corbels over the front door of Socknersh Manor

---

BURWASH

✳ ✳ ✳

COLLINS OF
SOCKNERSH

*Socknersh Manor,
which is in the parish
of Brightling, has been
altered and extended
from the time it
belonged to the Collins
family of ironmasters.
The first of them was
Alexander 'Collen' who
in his will of February
14 1547 left 'lands
and tenements at
Socknersse' to his
wife Julian.
Several of their
descendants are buried
in Brightling church,
on the north side of
the chancel where
space was reserved for
'the owners of the
manor house'.*

✳ ✳ ✳

Literary connections

BURWASH is one of the most visited villages in Sussex because of the Kipling connection. The poet of Empire and writer of short stories was already world famous when, at the age of thirty-seven, he moved with his family from The Elms at Rottingdean to Bateman's to escape the intrusive attentions of his admiring public. His arrival put the village on the tourist map and it has remained there firmly ever since.

In his autobiography, *Something of Myself*, published posthumously, he describes his first sight of the house from the driving seat of his Locomobile steam car. 'We had seen an advertisement for her, and we reached her down an enlarged rabbit warren of a lane. At very first sight the Committee of Ways and Means said: "That's her! The Only She! Make an honest woman of her – quick!"' However that could not be done until September 1902 as the owner had let the grand old house, with the year 1634 carved above its stone porch, for twelve months.

When Kipling, his American wife Caroline and their two children, John and Elsie, moved in one of the first things he did was to plant the yew hedges that border the gardens to this day. He planned to farm the estate, which he extended to 300 acres with the acquisition of Rye Green and Park Mill, and adapted the watermill to generate electric light. He had help from an expert in doing so – none other than Sir Walter Willcocks who had designed the Aswan Dam on the Nile.

The new owner of Bateman's had many demands

Bateman's

on his time and his talent. He travelled extensively – visiting Canada to receive an honorary degree from McGill University at Montreal; going to Stockholm in 1907 as the first English recipient of the Nobel Prize for Literature.

'During the six months or so each year that we stayed in England, there was always the House and the land, and on occasions the Brook at the foot of our garden which would flood devastatingly,' he wrote in *Something of Myself*. 'As she supplied the water for our turbine, and as the little weir which turned her current into the little mill-race was of frail antiquity, one had to attend to her often and at once, and always as the most inconvenient moments'.

Rudyard Kipling died in 1936 and his widow, who had remained at Bateman's, four years later. In her will Caroline Kipling left the house to the nation, making it a condition that it would be opened to the public. Bateman's is administered by the National Trust and is open from April to the end of October. The study where Kipling wrote so many of his Sussex stories is as he left it, as are the other rooms that can be visited.

✻ ✻ ✻

WHO DID BUILD BATEMAN'S

Who built Bateman's is not known. Certainly ironmaster John Brittain lived there but he died in 1707, seventy three years after the date above the porch.
It is unlikely, unless he was rich in youth and lived to a great age, that he was the original owner. His gravestone in St Bartholomew's churchyard has been eroded by wind and weather and gives no clue to how old he was when he died.

✻ ✻ ✻

Volunteers have restored the watermill to corn grinding role and it has Bateman's flour for sale. Entrance for visitors to the house and gardens is not through the splendid wrought iron gates between the tall yew hedges Kipling planted, but from the car park which is approached by a long drive from Bateman's Lane, off the A265.

Although the most famous, Kipling was not the only literary figure to have lived in Burwash. An Oxford Professor of Poetry, James Hurdis, was curate at St Bartholomew's for six years from 1785 and drew on that experience when he wrote *The Village Curate*. In it he describes the house in Spring Lane, then called Frys or The Friars, in which he lived with three of his sisters.

> In yonder mansion reared by rustic hands,
> And deck'd with no superfluous ornament,
> Where use was all the architect proposed,
> And all the master wish'd. Which scarce a mile
> From village tumult, to the morning sun
> Turns its warm aspect, yet with blossom hung
> Of cherry and of peach. . .

The house, now Burwash Place, has been considerably extended and looks quite different today. It was until recently a residential retirement home.

A more local but no less eminent man of letters was another former curate, John Coker Egerton, author of *Sussex Folk and Sussex Ways*. He was Burwash's rector from 1867 until his death in 1888 and wrote affectionately about his parish, its history and the people in his care.

James Fleming, who described himself as an organist, harmonium-maker, hairdresser, barber, bookbinder and violinist, wrote the words and the music of the Burwash Carol which was sung during his lifetime – he died in 1872 – between the hours of 3am and 4am on Christmas morning

A before dawn chorus of the carol has not been heard in the village for many years, but it did not disappear for good. The original manuscript, which had only the treble and bass parts, was preserved by John Coker Egerton's widow and a copy of the sheet music was given to choirmaster John Worthley.

The carol has since been sung again in the village at Christmas, not at the uncivilised hour of 3am but as part of the afternoon service of Nine Lessons and Carols at St Bartholomew's church.

Churches old and new

TODAY only the tower remains of the small Norman church that was built around 1090 on the eastern corner of the High Street and Bell Alley, now also known as School Hill. It originally consisted of the tower, nave and chancel and was extended by the addition of a north aisle and a south aisle during the next 200 years. The first reference to its dedication to St Bartholomew is in the Charter by which Henry III granted Burwash a weekly market and a May fair.

Like so many of the county's ancient churches it was extended and heavily restored in Queen Victoria's reign. Its oldest memorial, in fact the earliest example of a Sussex iron grave slab in existence, is against the north wall at the east end of the south aisle – an area known by Daniel and Una in *Rewards and Fairies* as 'Panama Corner' because of the inscription on the slab. It was formerly on the floor above the tomb of Joan Collins, whose family were the owners of Socknersh Forge, and was worn down by the feet of the faithful over many hundreds of years. However, the inscription, in anachronistic Lombardic script, can still be deciphered. It reads:

Orate P Annema Jhone Collins

On the south wall of this aisle, at the western end, is an oval bronze plaque to the memory of Lieutenant John Kipling, the eighteen year old son of a famous father, who fell at the Battle of Loos when serving with the Second Battalion, Irish Guards.

❋ ❋ ❋

A LIGHT TO REMEMBER

The beam from the lantern shines out from the four arched windows of the war memorial.

❋ ❋ ❋

It was the first commissioned work of the eminent sculptor, Sir Charles Wheeler, who was president of the Royal Society of Arts from 1956 to 1966.

There are other memorials to the victims of wars. In the porch are eleven wooden crosses, all that could be recovered of the crosses placed temporarily on the graves of the Burwash men who died on the battlefields of France and Flanders.

In the tower are two bells which were added to the existing six by a churchwarden of St Bartholomew's, Clement Woodbine Parish, in 1949. One is a memorial to his son Charles, the captain of a Stirling bomber, who failed to return from his fifty-fourth Pathfinder mission. The second new bell bears the words:

> Hearing me remember well
> Burwash men who fought and fell.

On an island site at the entrance to the church-yard is the war memorial inscribed with the names of some hundred servicemen and the dates of their death. On the anniversary of each one the light in the lantern at the top of the memorial is switched on and, as the village has no street lighting, its bright beam is visible to all who pass by. For years, until his death in 1995, the light was turned on by Alby Waterhouse, one time gardener at Bateman's. Now the ceremony is performed by Alby's son, Richard.

A little grassed graveyard surrounded by trees and in its centre a memorial: 'To those who fell in the Great War 1914-18', is all that remains of the Roman Catholic community that flourished at Southover for some sixty years.

In 1890, to meet the religious requirements of her

St Joseph's Roman Catholic Church.

domestic staff and estate workers, Madame de Murietta, a member of a rich and noble Spanish banking family who lived at Southover Hall, built the Church of St Joseph on land in Holton Hill, Spring Lane, that she had given to the diocese of Southwark. Craftsmen and materials were brought over from Italy, regardless of expense, to create a red brick Gothic style building of great beauty to replace the tin shed that did duty as a school during the week and where mass was said on Sundays. But three years after its consecration the de Muriettas, who also owned Wadhurst Park where they on occasions entertained the Prince of Wales, later King Edward VII, were declared bankrupt.

At about the same time the Salesians, a teaching order founded in Turin by John Bosco, the 'boy saint', were looking for somewhere in England to found a novitiate. They took over the church and the spiritual needs of the Catholic community in the locality and built a seminary which, when the novitiate moved to near Oxford in 1921, became a boarding and day school for boys from five to fourteen years old. It flourished until 1951 when it succumbed, like so many other 'voluntary

※ ※ ※

FROM FORCE TO FORGE

In 1985 Burwash gained a blacksmith and lost its village police constable. After sixteen years in the job PC David Hedges handed in his bicycle, cape and tall helmet and returned to the trade to which he was apprenticed for seven years before joining police force.

aided' schools, to the changing conditions of the times and the 1944 Education Act. The novitiate returned, but through lack of vocations, was forced to leave again in the 1960s and the parish of St Joseph's was handed over to the diocese of Arundel and Brighton. The building that had housed the school and seminary with its indoor swimming pool, tennis courts and playing fields was on the market for a number of years before it was bought and converted first into holiday apartments and later into flats and apartments which were subsequently sold.

The diocese required the church to be demolished rather than become derelict or converted to secular use. Father John Chadwick, the parish priest, stayed on at the presbytery, holding mass on alternate Sundays at Southover and at the new church of Christ the King in Burwash High Street.

※ ※ ※

BUXTED

Location: On the A272 two miles north east
Uckfield.
Population: 3,071.
Station: In the High Street.
Car park: Church Road.

BUXTED is not at all the village it used to be before the 1830s when the parsonage, the inn, the forge, a shop, some cottages, stocks and a whipping post were clustered together around the church in Buxted Park. It is now a ribbon development of Victorian and later buildings alongside the A272 and a name made known to the shoppers of Britain by the Buxted Chicken Packing Company, one of the first firms to process and market frozen poultry.

Charles Cecil Cope Jenkinson, 3rd Earl of Liverpool, was responsible for changing the character and situation of the village. He became the owner of Buxted Park in 1810 when he married Julia Evelyn-Medley who had inherited the estate from her great uncle. She died four years later and the earl, in search of seclusion, decided to clear the villagers away from their too close proximity to Buxted Place, the brick built manor house completed by George Medley, a wealthy wine merchant, in the eighteen century.

He offered to build them new homes outside the boundary of the park, which he planned to extend. 'No' they said. 'We don't want to move.' But in the end they had to for their landlord, Lord Liverpool, refused to do any repairs and the old cottages collapsed.

Buxted Place has filled a variety of roles since then. Royalty – first the Duchess of Kent and Princess Victoria, later Queen Mary – has been entertained there; architect Basil Ionides restored it with fittings from some war damaged stately homes after a fire in the 1940s; it housed an expensive health hydro in the 1960s and in 1972 was sold to Sheik Zayed,

41

* * *

THE DESIGN OF THE SIGN

*Buxted's village sign
(see page 41),
was put up in 1965 to
mark the golden
jubilee of the National
Federation of Women's
Institutes.
It was Enid Purvis's
winning design in a
WI competition and
shows a beech tree,
beneath which is a buck,
a cannon and the
Hogge rebus.
The WI symbol is on
the top of the wrought
iron sign which was
made at the Landon
Forge, Jarvis Brook.*

* * *

president of the United Arab Emirates and ruler of Abu Dhabi, who used it as his official residence until 1987. It was then bought by the Electric, Electronic, Telecommunication and Plumbing Union (EETPU) which planned to convert it into a holiday centre for its members. A few years ago it changed ownership again and was run by the Juldis Public Development Company of Bangkok as Buxted Park Country House Hotel. On December 1 1997 the forty-four bedroom mansion, complete with health club, gymnasium, saunas, steam rooms, heated out-door pool, five conference rooms and a cinema for presentations, was bought by Virgin Hotels.

At the entrance to the 326 acres of Buxted Park, off the A272 opposite the school, is the black and white timbered Hogge House, on the wall of which is the date 1581 and the rebus of Ralph Hogge. He is credited with making the first cast iron cannon in England, a process in which he was assisted by a Frenchman, Peter Baude, at Huggett's Forge in 1543.

Lord Liverpool removed the village but not its church. St Margaret the Queen was built in Buxted Park *c* 1250 and until the early nineteenth century served a huge parish which included Uckfield, Hadlow Down and Crowborough.

The dedication is an unusual one. Margaret was the second wife of Malcolm who succeeded to the Scottish throne on the demise of the Macbeths. She died in 1093, three days after hearing of the death of her husband and eldest son during yet another invasion of England by the Scots.

Queen Margaret was in character and conduct the exact opposite of Shakespeare's Lady Macbeth. *The Anglo Saxon Chronicles* says of her: 'She set the king right from the path of error, and turn him to the better way, and his people as well, and put down the evil customs the people had practised, just as she afterwards did.' Not surprisingly, after this write up, in 1249 the subject of it was canonised.

In the chancel, under the carpet by the altar rails, is one of the few cross fleury brasses not to have been destroyed by Cromwell's followers after the Civil War. It is a memorial to a former rector, Britellus Avenel, who died in 1408. On the wall by the font there is a framed rubbing of the brass, which is nearly seven feet long and has at its corners the symbols of the evangelists – a man, a lion, an ox and an eagle.

Another former rector, the Reverend Dr Christopher Wordsworth, brother of the Poet Laureate, lies in the churchyard. Buxted now has a second church, St Mary's in Church Road, which was built in 1884.

The entrance to the Hermit's Cave.

✳ ✳ ✳

A VINEYARD
ON THE
ROCKS

*Vines were once
grown beneath the
Hermitage Rocks
and a local name for
the area was The
Vineyard.
They were cultivated
in the 1820s by a
Mr Lidbetter, then
the tenant of
Rocks Farm.*

✳ ✳ ✳

The village's connection with the rearing, fattening
and processing of poultry, which began with the
arrival of the London, Brighton and South Coast
Railway's line from Lewes to London in 1858, ended
a few years ago when and the Buxted Chicken
Packing Company left its factory in Framfield Road
and moved to Five Ash Down where it now trades as
Grampian Country Foods. The former factory site has
been developed for sheltered and private housing.

On the rocks

BUXTED was a place of excursion for the curious
towards the end of the nineteenth century. What they
came to see were the caves in the rock formations that
give Rocks Lane its name. One, called the Hermit's
Cave, has a hall and living room with steps cut into
the rock to give access to an upper room. Another,

44

which looks like a turret, was called the Smugglers' Rock as the gangs of freebooters used it to store their contraband goods. The tenant of Rocks Farm, a Mr Lidbetter, was cultivating vines in the vicinity in the 1820 and using the caves to store his farm implements.

Nothing is known about the early occupants of these rock shelters but when an oast house and some cottages there were being converted into a house, appropriately called The Hermitage, a large grave was discovered in the sandstone on top of the rock strata of the Hastings beds. In it was a human skeleton – perhaps of the hermit who carved out a home in the cave?

Off Fowley Lane – surely a name that has something to do with chickens – is a track on the right leading to what little remains of Huggett's Forge where the famous first cannon was cast.

Almost opposite the station in Buxted is Framfield Road off which branches Nan Tuck's Lane, named after a woman from Rotherfield suspected of poisoning her husband by witchcraft. Nan, so the story goes, fled from her accusers towards Buxted church to claim sanctuary by touching the altar. She was running as fast as she could but her pursuers were gaining on her and were almost at her heels as she turned into a wood by the roadside – and vanished. Another ending to the tale is that she was caught and hanged in Tuck's Wood.

And there is a sequel. When the wood was re-planted after the First World War there was one patch in it where nothing would grow. . .

Crowborough Beacon, which was fired in 1988 to mark the 400th anniversary of the defeat of the Armada, and, below, the Goldsmiths' Leisure Centre.

CROWBOROUGH

Location: On the A26 eleven miles north of Uckfield.
Population: 19,120.
Car parks: Croft Road, north side of the High Street and Pine Grove.
Station: At Jarvis Brook.

C ROWBOROUGH, now the largest town in the North Wealden district, was a name long before it was a settlement of any size. In a deed of 1292 two acres of land 'in the waste of Crohbergh' (from the Old English *crawe beorg*, a mound frequented by crows) were granted by the then Archbishop of Canterbury, John Peckham, for a chapel and cemetery to replace an existing chapel which occupied one acre.

From then, until the mid eighteenth century, Crowborough rarely gets a mention. No one took much interest in this barren tract of the forest ridge. No baron built a castle there, no nobleman administered a manor.

Its height – the beacon is 796ft above sea level – deterred early settlers. They preferred to graze their cattle and raise their crops in the fertile valleys where there were rivers to provide means of transport. Only those seeking isolation from reasons of faith or felony – the hermits, wrongdoers fleeing justices, poachers and smugglers with contraband from the coast – chose to live in this wild and lawless wasteland.

Their names are not known, their graves are unmarked, but they left behind them a load of legends, a number of which are recounted by Boys Firman, a barrister living and writing in Crowborough in 1890. 'All . . . were related to me by old people still living in Crowborough,' he states, and proceeds to list a number of ghostly apparitions, some positively benevolent, some malevolent and one distinctly odd.

There is the apparition of a white-haired old man which appeared on the stairs of a house in Lye Green Road and pointed a ghostly finger at a flagstone on the floor beneath which the terrified householder later found a box of money. And a ghost who disturbed the sleep of the occupant of an old house on Hurtis Hill and beckoned him to follow it.

***

BLACKSMITH CHASED BY BAG OF SOOT

The most unorthodox of all the hauntings is the ghostly bag of soot which would chase any wayfarer who crossed Jarvis Brook Road A blacksmith, made brave with beer, declared the sootbag would not frighten him and climbed the hill to challenge it. Moments later he was seen by his drinking companions fleeing down the hill followed, at about shoulder height, by the bag of soot.

The soot bag, it was said, was carried by an unseen chimney sweep, angry at householders doing him out of a job by cleaning their own chimneys by setting fire to them.

***

One night he did so and was led to a small mound in a meadow which he dug into next day and discovered an iron pot full of gold and silver coins.

The ghost of a smuggler whose head was shot off by a gamekeeper is said to haunt the Warren estate. He roams the hill on horseback, carrying a lantern, and appears to be searching for something. His head, perhaps? Another headless ghost runs backwards and forwards across the road at Boarshead, and the sylph like figure of a woman used to haunt the Walshes, floating from the house to the gate in Jarvis Brook Road.

Ironmaster's investment

THE first person to show any concern for and interest in the occupants of this wild area was Sir Henry Fermor, an iron master who lived in Sevenoaks but had been born – on June 23 1677 – at the once-moated manor of Walshes which had been in his family for centuries. He died in 1734 and left £9,000 for a chapel and a school 'in or near a place called Crowborough. . . for the use of the very ignorant and heathenish people'.

He stipulated how the cash was to be divided between the building works, the salaries of the minister and schoolmaster and 'books, wool and hemp' for the scholars whose numbers were not to exceed forty at any one time. And he gave the trustees seven years to execute his instructions, which they did not do, and the matter was referred to the High Court.

Today nothing remains of the benefactor's birthplace. The old timber-framed Walshes Manor at Jarvis Brook burnt down in the early hours of

The school house, now the vicarage, and the chapel, now the parish church.

February 27 1893 and a larger house has since been built on the site.

Since medieval times civilisation, such as it was, had been passing Crowborough by to the west, on what is now the A26. In the sixteenth century an enterprising alewife opened an inn at the second crossroads going south from Tunbridge Wells to Lewes and in the coaching days of Georgian England it came to be called the Red Cross Inn for it was marked by a red cross on what passed for a road map in those days.

Four coaches a week clattered along this road, their drivers referring frequently to a three inch wide strip of material, mounted on rollers, which showed the full length of the road with location points marked with symbols in different colours. A mile on from the Red Cross Inn, now the Cross, is the Blue Anchor named, perhaps, from another symbol on the same map.

Enter an entrepreneur

IN 1809 Crowborough had its first commuter – but from the capital to the country rather than the other way round. Edward Howis, a dealer in oils in London's Piccadilly, leased Crowborough Warren estate and

✻ ✻ ✻

FLOUR FOR THE
QUEEN'S
WEDDING CAKE

*IT was on the New
Mill, with its 30ft
wheel, that the
flour for Queen
Victoria's wedding
cake was ground.
From Crowborough
it was delivered
to the Berkeley
Square premises of
Gunter, the London
confectioner who
was to make the
cake – and to whose
daughter Edward
Howis's son was
engaged.*

✻ ✻ ✻

immediately embarked on an extensive scheme of improvements which provided much needed jobs for the people of the area.

He planted stands of birch and beech, silver firs and towering pines over several hundred of its 1,400 acres; enclosed sections with banks and hedges; made two large ponds and built two watermills, numerous outbuildings and a house for his own occupation.

Edward Howis would leave London daily in the early hours of the morning and ride or drive the forty or more miles to Crowborough, arriving in time for breakfast. After spending the day supervising work on the estate, he would return to London in the evening, changing horses at Godstone as he had done on the outward journey.

He was a great organiser. To get the chalk he needed for his estate roads he had it brought by barge along the River Ouse from Lewes to Shortbridge. From there it was collected by a team of twelve donkeys, harnessed two abreast to small waggons. Three times a week, with their harness bells jingling, the animals would do the sixteen mile round trip.

Corn continued to be ground at the New Mill until the 1890s when the miller moved to smaller premises at Ore, near Hastings. The Old Mill on the estate was being used as a sawmill up to the start of the First World War.

Going for growth

IT was not until the 1880s that Crowborough began to grow. The arrival of the railway at Jarvis Brook in 1868 and the publication by Dr Charles Leeson

Prince of his *Observations on the Climate and Topography of Crowborough Hill, Sussex* sparked off the first period of expansion.

The doctor, a great believer in the beneficial effects of fresh air, had retired from his father's practice in Uckfield in 1872 and moved first to a house called the Grange on top of the Beacon and then to The Observatory, now flats, which he had built in Church Road. From there he made the meteorological and geological observations which form the basis of the book which he distributed free to doctor friends and colleagues throughout the country.

It had an almost immediate effect. In his introduction to the second edition, published in 1898, he was able to write of Crowborough, with understandable pride: 'A great transformation has come over the scene in the last twenty years and it is rapidly becoming one of the most favoured health resorts in the South of England; nor can this be a matter for surprise when we take into consideration the remarkable purity of the air on the Hill, abounding as it does in ozone and other valuable

A house in the country – on the Crowborough Warren estate today.

Crowborough Golf Club – now one of the finest inland courses in the country.

❈ ❈ ❈

ROOMS WITH A VIEW

A short walk from the golf course was the newly built Beacon Hotel with 'superior accommodation for the many persons who may require a short sojourn here to enjoy the splendid view and delightful air which may be obtained at the golf links'.

❈ ❈ ❈

atmospheric constituents. . . Few indeed are the invalids who do not quickly derive benefit from even a short sojourn in the immediate neighbourhood.'

Senior Civil Servants and officers of the armed forces were among the first to build imposing homes for their retirement on those parts of Ashdown Forest that had been enclosed and cleared some 200 years previously. At about the same time the Goldsmiths' Company bought a number of estates in the neighbourhood, revived their farms, and let them to rich City merchants seeking country homes for shooting parties and healthy holidays.

On October 5 1895 Lady Cantelupe was handed a club, and in the pouring rain, with her husband holding an umbrella over her, drove the first ball to open the nine hole golf course created on 220 acres of the Manor of Alchornes. Her father-in-law, Earl de la Warr, who was lord of the manor, had given the club a twenty five year lease of the land at a peppercorn rent of five shillings a year. Two years later the course was extended to eighteen holes and today it is one of the finest inland golf courses in England.

The arrival of monied men of leisure with their families and friends not only benefitted the builders and tradesmen in the area but also the small communities of the near destitute that had been trying to scratch a living by poaching, smuggling and cutting heather for bedding from the otherwise barren Common.

Dr Leeson Prince had first hand experience of just how poor were the poor. One winter's night he was called to a patient who needed his constant attention at the bedside. Wondering why his feet were getting so cold he looked down and found they were covered with snow that had blown in through a broken window.

'This was not the only inconvenience experienced by the household,' he wrote, 'for in consequence of the inclement weather my horse was brought into the kitchen where, being left to its own devices, it found out the bread crock and devoured its contents.' Another family the doctor visited he found eating some turnip rinds. On inquiring what else they had he received the reply: 'Nothing, we had the turnips yesterday.' There was no bread in the house and to drink they only had 'hot water stained with tea, for it really was nothing more.'

New parish, new people

CROWBOROUGH became an ecclesiastical parish in 1880. Before that it had no independent existence but was part of Rotherfield. The chapel that was Sir Henry Fermor's bequest was rebuilt, except for the tower which was retained, into the present church of All Saints in 1883 and extended again, at a cost of £2,000, in 1898. The civil parish came into being in April 1905.

The area was advertised by estate agents and by illustrations in the first class carriages of the London, Brighton and South Coast Railway, as the Scotland of Sussex and among the first to move there for his health

Downs House, where Richard Jeffries lived for a few months and, below,
Windlesham, where the creator of Sherlock Holmes lived for twenty-three years.

was the naturalist Richard Jefferies, author of *Bevis,The Story of a Boy* and a strange, mystical autobiography, *Story of My Heart*.

For a few months before his death in 1887 he lived in a stone cottage called The Downs, still on the left hand side of London Road. It has recently been restored and above its front door is a sign commemorating its occupation by this great observer of nature. Boys Firman recalled meeting Jefferies on his walks through the fields and lanes of the Weald. 'He was then sick unto death, for an insidious disease was hurrying him to the grave,' he wrote. 'He was not understood at Crowborough. He did not come with a full purse, but with a rich mind only.'

Crowborough did, however, take pride in Jack Russell Lambert, all 2ft 10inches of him. Jackie, born in 1898 in a house in Queens Road, weighed 27lbs and was said to be the smallest man in England. Later he moved with his brother, Harry and his sister-in-law to Guildford Lodge in Eridge Road, near the Red Cross Inn, of which he became regular patron. He would walk about in the sporting tweeds, stock and gaiters of a country squire and if asked to pose for picture postcards or to appear at local sports and fairs, would don the uniform of a naval officer. When he died in 1936, at the age of thirty-eight, the whole of Crowborough came to a halt for his funeral procession.

The next renowned writer to take up residence was Sir Arthur Conan Doyle, the creator of Sherlock Holmes. He moved in 1907 with his second wife, Jean Leckie, into Little Windlesham in Hurtis Hill, quite close to the house in Lordswell Lane in which the Leckie family spent many holidays. He extended it considerably, adding a large billiards room and music room, building a summerhouse in the garden and dropping the 'Little' from 'Windlesham' on his writing paper.

Conan Doyle soon settled into Crowborough society. He became captain of the Beacon Golf Club in 1910 and regularly played over the course until rheumatism restricted the amount of exercise he cared to take. The three children of his second marriage were all born at Windlesham and went for a time to schools in Crowborough. He employed local people, patronised the local shops and during the First World War formed the Civil Reserve, a branch of the First Battalion of

THE CASE OF THE CHICKEN RUN MURDER

SIR ARTHUR offered his services to Scotland Yard when there was a murder virtually on his doorstep.
The dismembered body of Elsie Cameron, a London typist, was found buried beneath a chicken run at a poultry farm in Luxford Lane.
Chicken farmer Norman Thorne, to whom Elsie was engaged, was tried, convicted and hanged for her murder.
He claimed he had found Elsie's body hanging from a beam in his barn and had panicked, cut the body into bits, and buried it.

* * *

Volunteers which became part of the Sixth Royal Sussex Volunteer Regiment.

Between the wars house guests at Windlesham included many of the literary lions of the day, among them Sir James Barrie, Bernard Shaw and H G Wells. Rudyard Kipling would come over from Bateman's at Burwash, Rider Haggard from his brother's house in St Leonards. With H Ashton Wolfe of the Paris Sureté, William J Burns of the Burns Detective Agency in the USA, and Sir Edward Marshall Hall, the most admired advocate of his day, he would delight in discussing crime and methods of detection. Arctic explorer Sven Svenson would spread out his maps on the green baize of the billiards table and plan his next voyage.

Sir Arthur Conan Doyle died of a heart attack on July 7 1930 and was buried in the garden of Windlesham. The grave marker was of oak and bore the words 'steel true and blade safe.' On either side of it were carved lifelike hands, one clutching a steel sword and the left one holding a metal flaming torch. His wife, who died in 1940, was buried beside him. After the Second World War, during which various regiments were stationed at Windlesham, the house was sold and the bodies exhumed and reburied in the churchyard at Minstead in the New Forest.

Crowborough then seemed to forget the writer who, for twenty-three years, had brought it some recognition and reward. Windlesham became Windlesham Manor, a registered residential care home. It has retained a few links with its previous owner – his portrait still hangs in the room at the rear of the billiards room, now the residents' lounge and dining room, and the stag's head on which he hung his bandoleer from the Boer War is still over the fireplace.

Suddenly, a few years ago, Crowborough began to flaunt its Conan Doyle connections, no doubt for good commercial reasons. Signs on the roads into the town, which had previously just announced its name, now appear with the words:

CROWBOROUGH
Home of Sir Arthur Conan Doyle

A memorial museum to house the Conan Doyle (Crowborough) Establishment Collection of photographs and ephemera which had been on display in the Cross Hotel, was opened in Groombridge Place on the Kent/Sussex borders in 1995 and the following year the first Sherlock Holmes Festival was held. Its intention was to honour the memory of Sir Arthur, support mystery writing and attract visitors to the area. It did, in fact, attract 23,000 visitors and they came from all parts of the world, including a number of Holmes enthusiasts from Japan, and a commemorative plaque to the famous author was placed with some ceremony on the west wall of Waitrose.

The war years – and after

* * *

MISS PRINT?

Sixty-four year old Miss Haskins must have been amazed and amused to find herself described by one London daily newspaper on its billboards as:

CROWBOROUGH
VILLAGE
GIRL
POETESS.

* * *

FOR a few days after Christmas 1939 the attention of the world's press was focused on Crowborough. Reporters with notebooks and photographers with plate cameras were on the hunt for retired London School of Economics lecturer Minnie Louise Haskins, inadvertently made an instant celebrity by King George VI when he ended his first wartime Christmas Day broadcast with a verse of her poem entitled God Knows:

And I said to the man that stood at the gate of the year
'Give me a light that I may tread safely into the unknown.'
And he replied, 'Go out into the darkness and put your hand
into the hand of God,
That shall be better than light and safer than a known way.'

These words touched the heart of the nation and immediately everybody wanted to know all about the poet whose only self published work at that time was a collection of religious verses, among them *God Knows*, which appeared in 1930. But Miss Haskins valued her privacy. She gave very few interviews to the reporters who crowded round Brooklands in Ghyll Road, where she had lived for fourteen years with her two sisters, and she allowed few biographical details in the ninety-page book of her poems *The Gate of the Year*, published by Hodder and Stoughton in 1940 and reprinted six times.

The press were in Crowborough again in 1955, with an equal lack of success. Their quarry this time was British diplomat Kim Philby who had been named as the Third Man in the Burgess-McLean spy scandal. He had gone to ground in his house in Aviemore Road, Crowborough and managed to avoid his pursuers by breakfasting early and spending the day in Ashdown Forest.

And he was lucky that the press had other, more compelling, interests in the neighbourhood. The Princess Margaret/Group Captain Peter Townsend romance was at the 'will they, won't they marry' stage and the couple were staying some six miles away with Lord and Lady Rupert Nevill at Uckfield House. The reporters would converge on Philby's house around lunchtime, leaving the royal romance for an hour or two, but never found him at home.

With so many retired members of the armed forces among its residents it is not surprising that the area was virtually under military occupation throughout the war. Its terrain made it an ideal training area for tanks and troops and regiment after regiment passed through the camp set up on land near the Warren and, in preparation for D Day, spent time under canvas on the Common. It was on the golf course there, in June 1944, that three soldiers in the Welland and Lincoln Regiment were killed by a flying bomb. Crowborough Training Camp never closed. It is used today by the Regular Army and the Territorials for training purposes.

The building boom of the immediate post war years created the Crowborough of the 1990s. Well planned housing estates went up amid the avenues of detached houses with grounds of the earlier incomers and, in a few years the population rose from 6,000 or so to around 11,000. Today it is 20,000 – and counting.

The new residents were the young, upwardly mobile, rather than the rich retired. They wanted a good train service to London, where most of them worked, schools for their children, a variety of shops and services, and some sports facilities for all the family. Now they have them – and plenty of healthy fresh air as well. Dr Leeson Prince and Sir Henry Fermor, the first to invest in the area, would have been pleased.

DALLINGTON

Location: Six miles south west of Robertsbridge,
left off the B2096
Population: 319.
Station: Robertsbridge

*This splendid yew
hedge in the shape
of an H for hostelry
is at the gate of a
house called Yew
Arch, opposite
the steps leading to
the church.
It has been grown to
show that the house
behind it was once a
beerhouse called
the George.*

* * *

MOST of the the history of this pretty village happened some 800 years ago. The manor of Dallington, which was extensive, was valued at £80 a year in 1106 when it was handed over by Henry I to four burgesses of Caen as a reward to them for surrendering the town to him when he was campaigning to get Normandy back from his brother, Robert.

A 20yd length of wall, parts of it 10ft high, and some massive buttresses in the grounds of Oldcastle in Prinkles Lane are relics of the private wars waged between the barons when the country was in chaos after the death of King Henry I. They formed part of an adulterine or unlicensed castle, one of a hundred built throughout the country when Stephen and Matilda were struggling for the throne of England, and date from around 1130, when the manor of Dallington was in the hands of a Norman knight, William de St Leger.

It was he, or his second son William of Socknersh, who fortified the hunting box on the edge of the royal forest of Dallington which still extends over many hundreds of acres to the north and west of the village.

The Oldcastle of today – a house restored in 1910 in the Tudor style by architect Sir Eric Newton for Lord Wrenbury – is still surrounded by a splendid stone wall but one dating from Edwardian rather than Plantagenet times.

Dallington is as unusual ecclesiastically as it is historically. It has been a rural deanery in the Archdeaconry of Lewes since the twelfth century and currently has jurisdiction over some twenty parishes, including such sizeable places as Mayfield and Hailsham.

For nine years from 1988 Canon David Fricker was both vicar and Rural Dean of Dallington. The present rural dean is the rector of Hailsham and the Rector of Brightling, the Reverend Stuart Baker, now

looks after the spiritual needs of Dallington, Mountfield and Netherfield. However, the village is not without a resident priest, in fact it has two non-stipendiaries – Lord John Wrenbury of Oldcastle and Jane Sherwin.

There is some doubt about the dedication of the church. Should it be to St Margaret or St Giles, as is it currently called? Those who favour St Margaret of Antioch – and they include Sussex historian Mark Anthony Lower – quote a Hastings Priory charter of 1180-1204 which refers to 'the church of St Margaret' at Dallington; a 1291 papal taxation; and that the annual parish fair was held on St Margaret's Day, July 20.

The first mention of St Giles, patron saint of beggars and lepers, is in the parish registers of 1643. His cause is championed by Miss

✳ ✳ ✳

ROADSIDE
REMEMBRANCE

A cross by the roadside at Padgham Corner in Hammer's Lane, near Southview Farm, marks the spot where Flying Officer Peter Crofts landed when his Hurricane was shot down in a dogfight over the Dallington on September 28 1940. The memorial is looked after by Heathfield Royal Air Forces Association and it holds a service of commemoration there every year.

✳ ✳ ✳

Adelaide Tatham, daughter of a former rector, who argues in her *Records of the Parish of Dallington* that the original church on the site was dedicated to St Giles and it was rebuilt in the fourteenth century by Sir Thomas Hooe, who had obtained the charter for the fair, and dedicated to St Margaret.

A second rebuilding of the church caused even more controversy. The Earl of Ashburnham was its patron and he was totally against the old church being demolished although his architect had reported that it was in a dangerous state.

The Earl was not convinced and took his case to the Consistory Court at Lewes. He lost. In 1864 St Margaret's or St Giles was rebuilt with Victorian vigour, only its fifteenth century tower and stone spire escaping the attention of the restorers.

Dallington still has a school – the old one, built of grey Ashburnham brick, is now the village hall – a shop and an inn. Today not all of them are by the church as they used to be. The inn is the Swan at Woods Corner and near to it, on the B2096, is Dallington general stores and post office.

ETCHINGHAM

Location: On the A265 two and a half miles east of
Burwash.
Population: 738.
Station: In the High Street.

THE new has ousted most of the old in this main road village. Its present day attraction is its railway station – a building of golden stone with smart red and blue doors and the railings of its footbridge picked out in white with bright red handrails. Passengers come by car, bus and bicycle from as far away as Heathfield to the west and villages of Kent to the east creating a Monday to Friday morning and evening rush hour of quite impressive proportions. And since CCTV has been installed in the station's pay and display car park there has been a big drop in the number of thefts from commuters' cars.

The church nearly collapsed through subsidence in 1937 and evidence of the amount of underpinning necessary to save it can be seen on the tower.

The railway arrived at Etchingham in 1851 and brought with it a minor building boom. Old cottages were replaced by a ribbon development of Victorian houses and the Eagle 'commercial inn and posting house' on the east side of the level crossing provided horse drawn cabs for passengers arriving by train. By 1874 it had competition from the new Station Hotel next to the post office. That burnt down around 1910 but was rebuilt and re-opened first as the Railway Hotel, and later the name was changed to the de Echynham Arms. The Eagle became the Temperance Hotel, selling sweets and cups of tea to travellers until it closed in the late 1940s. The de Echynham Arms was the last to close and houses are about to be built on the site.

Almost hidden by trees, on land to the east of the station, is the church Sir William de Echynham re-built in honour of the Assumption of the Blessed Virgin and St Nicholas in 1360. Its sheet copper vane, the oldest one in the country still in position, has been patched and repaired a number of times since it was placed on the spire. It bears Sir William's arms – on a field azure fretty in six pieces – a design which is repeated, in more simple form, on the village sign (see page 63).

An inscription on a brass of Sir William in armour in the chancel floor states, in Norman French, that he died on January 18 1387 'as it pleased God about midnight'. Another, in Latin, gives full details of the church's dedication.

On the south wall is a memorial to Henry Corbould, the designer of the Penny Black, the first British postage stamp. He was buried at Etchingham for no other reason than that he was 'seized with apoplexy when riding from St Leonards to Hurst Green on December 8 1844, and died ten hours later at Robertsbridge'.

Corbould, who had studied under Fuseli at the Royal Academy, was a Fellow of the Society of Antiquaries and spent years in the British Museum drawing the Elgin marbles. He was commissioned to draw the

* * *

HAMMER AND ANVIL HAVE VANISHED

For years the anvil and hammer from the forge at Etchingham were in the grounds of Lewes Castle, beside a section of railings forged in Sussex for St Paul's Cathedral.
The railings are still there but the hammer and anvil are not. However a working model of the forge can be seen in the Sussex Archeological Society's Anne of Cleves House Museum in Lewes.

* * *

young Queen Victoria in 1837 and it was from this drawing, for which he was paid £12, that the Penny Black was engraved.

Fortunately the church did not receive the attentions of Victorian restorers and most of its structure and furnishings are original. The choir stalls in the chancel all retain their misericords – the carved ledges under tip up seats which offered some support to the choristers during long services. Most are carved with foliage but the ones on the eastern sides show a fox dressed as a friar preaching to geese.

A depression in the ground in Queens Gardens is all that remains of the moat that surrounded the church in the days when the Rother – joined here by the Dudwell and Limden – was navigable to ships as far as Etchingham. The vessels carried iron from Sir Robert Tyrrwhitt's forge in the village, and forges at Hurst Green and Robertsbridge, to the port of Rye.

Restoration has removed much of the history from the manor houses in the area – and the entire old manor house of Etchingham, on the site of which the station now stands. The greatest recorded loss was at Haremere Hall where a whole roomful of fifteenth and early sixteenth century furniture was burnt as useless lumber. The room had remained untouched for 200 years – from the day in 1640 when, so the story goes, Colonel John Busbridge was shot by a patrol of Cromwell's troops as he leaned out of the west window of his bedroom to see who was approaching.

The bed, with arabesque decoration on its Tudor headboard similar to those at Knole and Hampton Court, had its covers thrown back as the colonel had left it. No one had touched the firedogs dating from the reign of Henry V; looked through a chestful of early papers; or noted the Cromwellian dates stamped on the leather seats of the oak chairs.

When artist Henry Corbould was staying at Haremere as a guest of the Sneppe family he made some drawings of the colonel's room and its contents. Later on, while the house was being restored for new owners, he asked them about preserving the room and the furniture in it – only to be told that it had all been thrown out.

Haremere Hall, now owned by the Killearn Estates, was one of the tourist attractions of the area when the Sussex Shire horses bred by Brenda and John Lavis were stabled there. Thousands came each year to see the magnificent animals and to get advice on how they could be used in present day agriculture. The Lavises retired in 1992 and their heavy horses are now with the Working Horse Trust at Forge Wood Farm, Eridge Green.

William's warhorse

IT was a Norman rather than a Sussex warhorse that William 1 had shod at Etchingham after the Battle of Hastings for he had brought 3,000 across the Channel on September 27 1066. The smith must have done a good job because, so it said, the king named the house where his horse was shod Shoyswell.

Shoyswell Manor, north west of Etchingham on the road to Stonegate, was owned by a family of that name until 1690 when Roger Shoyswell, a captain of the Trained Band – the local militia of those days – died. The three horseshoes on the family's coat of arms appear to confirm the farriery connection.

In his will of 1580 Thomas Shoyswell made some most extraordinary bequests to his wife, Dorothy. As well as the expected gifts of a man of substance, such a silver gilt cup and items of furniture including 'the chest that I made in Sheffyld' and 'the cubberd that standeth at my bede head', he left her 'the use and wering of her wedinge ring for lief', and a room in his house and the garret above it.

Perhaps by willing 'the Grene chamber, and the chamber within the

Old Shoyswell Manor.

* * *

THE PELHAM
BUCKLE

A buckle from the augmentation of honour granted to Sir John appears on the houses owned by the family, and on the fonts they gave to churches in the county

* * *

same' Sir Thomas was making sure his widow had somewhere to live and would not be cast out by his heirs. She was to have 'ingress and eggress and regresse into and from the same by the ways, droves and stayers used and accustomed to the same . . . and free liberty to bake and brewe in the bakehouse and brewhouse . . . and to drye her clothes uppon the hedges and bushes . . . and sufficient rome, pasture and haye for ii geldings in the stables and grounds here adjoyning the said mannor house'.

Another king from across the Channel lived at King's Lodge but John of France came as an exile rather than as a conqueror. He was captured by Sir John de Pelham at the Battle of Poitiers in 1356 and the buckles on the Pelham coat of arms are said to be those from the sword the king surrendered to his captor.

HADLOW DOWN

Location: On the A272 two and a half miles east of Buxted.
Population: 648.
Station: Buxted.

Squatters have been part of the social scene of the High Weald for centuries. When Hadlow Down became a parish in 1837 it took in the once desolate area round Spotted Cow Lane which had been 'colonised' by the workers at Howbourne forge, according to the custom that if a man could build a dwelling in twenty four hours he could claim the plot of unfenced land on which it stood and hold it in perpetuity.

Those who acquired their freeholds in this fashion were regulars at the Spotted Cow, an alehouse which flourished in the lane from the seventeenth century until it closed in 1900. It is now a private house called The Vatch, which keeps up the connection with a name plate showing white cows with black spots grazing on a green field.

St Mark's church with its thin, tapering spire, is the dominant feature of the roadside village of Hadlow Down. Which was perhaps the intention of Charles Lang Huggins of Hadlow Grange who had the original church on the site remodelled at his own expense by architect G Fellowes-Prynne in 1912.

The first St Mark's was built in 1836 on land given by Earl de la Warr for a church, vicarage and village school. It was designed by William Moseley and had small chancel, nave and square tower with a short spire. Today it has a tall shingled spire, and an extended chancel and Lady Chapel at the western end. Charles Huggins had inherited Hadlow Grange on the death of his father, stockbroker Thomas Huggins, who had enlarged the property considerably. *Kelly's Directory* of 1890 refers to 'C L Huggins JP' as one of the major landowners in the area – the other being the Marquis of Abergavenny – and lists among his gifts to the village 'a Home of Rest for the sisters of All Saints . . . serving as a holiday

St Margaret's church.

home in the summer months and a Working Men's Club for the rest of the year.'

Another place of worship which has been altered architecturally is the Calvinist Baptist chapel, built in 1849 with seating for about 500. When it opened on July 7 more than a thousand would-be worshippers turned up, some from as far afield as Petworth, and the windows were left open so they could hear, if not see, the service.

In 1987, when the chapel lost its roof in the storm, the congregation had dwindled to a handful and the trustees decided to sell it rather than restore it. They invested the proceeds in a trust fund, the income from which, under Charity Commission arrangements, is given in March each year to a needy chapel in the area. However, the trustees retained the small burial ground that surrounds the house recently built on the chapel site and keep it mown and well maintained.

The structural incongruities of the New Inn, pictured below, are, it is

＊＊＊

BLAZE BEATS
THE BAILIFFS

*An earlier New Inn
burnt down in the
1880s – not
accidentally, some say,
because the blaze
occurred just before
bailiffs arrived to seize
the landlord's
possessions.
He had run out of
both cash and
credit.*

＊＊＊

said, the responsibility of a Brighton church architect, Samuel Denman, who built it in 1887. Its other incongruities – it is next to a (now disused) scrapyard, has only one useable door, its opening hours can vary, it is not on the phone – attract rather than repel those who relish a peep into the past. And it is a favourite watering-hole for people attending the steam engine rallies held at nearby Tinkers Park.

South off the A272, down Wilderness Lane, was the large furnace of Pounsley and the remains of its dam on the Tickerage Stream can still be seen. Further upstream, at Pounsley Mill Farm, is the Gunbanks into which shot from the newly cast cannon was fired. A ball found there, bearing the government mark, was presented by C L Huggins to the Sussex Archeological Society in 1925.

A much older and odder feature is the acre of land surrounded by a much silted up 20ft wide moat. It lies to the north east of Shepherds Hill and is marked on post 1968 Ordnance Survey maps as an ancient monument. Various suggestions have been put forward to explain its purpose – one being that it was used as a safe haven from wolves for women and stock when the men were away from the settlement on hunting expeditions. Excavations have produced a quantity of thirteenth century green zigzag patterned glazed pottery but no earlier artefacts.

Stables for sixteen horses with a fine arched entrance for his coach were built at Shepherds Hill in 1740 by Sir Robert Fagg. He died a year later, before work had started on the house he intended to go with these outbuildings. It was left to the architect of Guildford Cathedral, Sir Gerald Maufe, to complete the project. In 1926 he bought the stable block and converted the existing farm buildings behind it into a house and lived there until his death in 1974, at the age of ninety-one.

A hamlet comes and goes

FIVE ASHES, a hamlet recorded under that name in 1512, was originally in the parish of Hadlow Down. The clump of ash trees after which it was called were on a bank on the west side of the road which is now the A267. They were grubbed out in the 1860s so that a post office and shop could be built there and for a time Five Ashes, which is now in the parish of Mayfield, was ash-less.

William Pettit had planted five limes outside his inn in 1892 to commemorate his five daughters but it was not until 1912 that the five ashes given by Mr Nicolson of Skippers Hill Manor were planted by a later landlord, Alfred Berwick, on the green opposite the inn. They, like their predecessors, were tall, handsome trees when they were felled in 1987 – not this time by the hand of man but by the hurricane. Their sapling replacements are growing well.

HEATHFIELD

HEATHFIELD

Location: On the A265 at the eastern end of the
southern forest ridge. Cade Street is on the B2096 to
Battle.
Population: 10,676.
Station: Buxted, six and a half miles east.
Car parks: High Street and Station Road.

*One of the Sussex
rites of spring, the
releasing of a cuckoo
from a basket, belongs
by tradition to
Heathfield, hence the
design on the village
sign.
Horse trading gipsies
from all over the south
gathered at Cade Street
for the annual spring
market. To mark the
start of the wheeling
and dealing an old
gipsy women would
release a cuckoo from a
basket. Someone gave
her the name Dame
Heffle – a contraction of
Heathfield – and it
caught on to such an
extent that the market
became known
as the Heffle Fair.*

* * *

THERE is Heathfield and there is Old Heathfield.
They are separated by centuries, and by the
walled acres of Heathfield Park. Old
Heathfield, which extends into Cade Street, formerly
Catte or Carter's Street, has a church with a list of vic-
ars dating from 1400 and an inn, the Star, which started as an alehouse for the stonemasons building the
original Norman church.

A vicar of All Saints, Old Heathfield, accompanied
by a few regulars from the Star, sailed away to the
New World in 1606. Thirty-seven year old Robert
Hunt had been chosen by the Archbishop of
Canterbury 'as an honest, religious and courageous
divine' to go with Richard Hakluyt on his expedition
to discover new lands across the sea. He was the first
clergyman to settle in America and there is a plaque
to his memory in the Star, given by the American
and British Commonwealth Association of the
United States in 1957. It commemorates the 350th
anniversary of the founding of the first permanent
English settlement in North America, at Jamestown,
Virginia.

There is also a memorial window to him in All
Saints Church. It was given by Dawn Langley
Simmons in memory of her grandmother and great

aunt – twin sisters Nellie and Clara Ticehurst who lived in Old Heathfield – and unveiled in 1962 by her adoptive mother, that great English comedy actress, Dame Margaret Rutherford. The twin arched window shows Robert Hunt celebrating Holy Communion before a congregation of settlers and native Americans. The two Red Indian children have the faces of the Ticehurst twins – copied by the artist Laurence Lee from a photograph of them on the beach at Brighton.

Dawn was registered at birth as Gordon Langley Hall, for the midwife declared the baby was a boy. After some minor corrective surgery in America as an adult Gordon became Dawn and later married and had a daughter, Natasha. She is now a grandmother, and still writing.

Fattening the Surrey fowl

IT was at Cade Street in the 1780s that the Sussex chicken fattening industry started – and poultry for the table has been having a hard time ever since

Kezia Collins of Keeper's Cottage, Cade Street is credited with being the first to develop commercially the hand cramming of chicken with a mixture of milk, fat and dried oats. A machine was invented to do the job and loads of Surrey fowl would arrive lean and alive by road and rail – leaving three to four weeks later plump, dead and dusted with flour.

By the 1930s Heathfield fatteners were dealing with a million birds a year – representing a £500,000 cash crop on the wholesale market. They would be brought in daily by the

The cramming machine in operation.

75

✳ ✳ ✳

WHERE CADE
WAS CAPTURED

The inscription on the stone beside the B2100, whick marks the spot where Cade was captured reads more like a warning than a memorial – which was probably Newberry's intention.

'This is the success
of all rebels
and this
future chanceth to
all traitors.'

lorry load from fatteners in villages in the vicinity and transferred at the Crown Hotel to a large lorry for London or taken to the station to catch the goods train known as the Chicken Express. Some two tons a year also went by passenger train. Force feeding as a method of fattening was finished off after the war by the introduction of caponising tablets and a change to battery farming.

When Mrs Collins started the cramming industry Cade Street was Catte's Street. It was not until 1792, when Francis Newberry of Heathfield Park erected a stone near the Half Moon on the spot where, it is said, the rebel Jack Cade was captured by Alexander Iden, the Sheriff of Kent, that the name was changed to Cade Street. Cade died from the wounds as he was being carried on a cart back to London where his body was drawn and quartered and his head fixed to the ramparts of the Tower.

Newberry had no admiration for Jack Cade, an Irishman who marched on London at the head of 20,000 men in 1450 to demand a fairer deal for farm labourers and for government reform.

However, he regarded General George Eliot, in quite a different light. And with good reason. The Defender of Gibraltar, popularly known as the Cock o' the Rock, had become the hero of the British people for holding out for three years with a small garrison against the naval and military might of France and Spain. He was raised to the peerage by a grateful government and took the title of Lord Heathfield from the village where he had lived since 1766 when he bought the William and Mary mansion, then called Bayley Park, with some of the prize money he had received for his part in the capture of Havana.

In his employ there, as his staff foreman, was the Apostle of Sussex, George Gilbert, a soldier who, having found religion, embraced the cause of non-conformity and preached about it with evangelistic ardour in all the new chapels in the vicinity. Gilbert, with the help of the General Eliot, was able to obtain his discharge from the army. He became a minister and founded the first chapel to occupy the site of the present Independent Chapel on the B2096 between Cade Street and Punnett's Town.

When Newberry bought Bayley Park two years after the death of its famous owner he built a 55ft high tower in the north-west corner of the park and had the words *Calpes Defensori* – To the Defender of Gibraltar – set up over its door in letters made of metal from Spanish guns used in the siege. It cost him £3,000, a sum which this successful publisher, dealer in patent medicines and liveryman of the Goldsmiths' Company could easily afford.

The next owner to make a lasting impression on the park was Sir Charles Blunt. Partly to protect his boundaries but also to provide work for a local labour force then in desperate need, he had a three and a half mile wall built round its 350 acres. The job was undertaken in 1833 by Michael Harmer, a close relative of Jonathan Harmer, the Heathfield sculptor whose terracotta plaques appear in so many East Sussex churchyards. It took him and his workers three years to complete.

The Gibraltar Tower

77

Heathfield Park and, below, the Independent Chapel that now occupies the site of the one built by George Gilbert.

A change of character rather than of construction came 140 years later when the gates of Heathfield Park, previously kept as a very private place by successive owners, were flung open to the great British public. by surgeon, dentist and dilettante Dr Gerald Moore. He bought the estate and set up a wildlife park at the western end.

The Gibraltar Tower was changed from an ivy covered remain to a museum of exhibits commemorating General Eliot; there was a pool for the sea lions; an aviary of exotic birds; and animals of all kinds in enclosures. For a time it was a successful tourist attraction but there were problems with planning permission and complaints from residents about traffic congestion and escaping animals. On one occasion fifteen kangaroos got away and did no good to gardens in the vicinity. There was a collective sigh of relief from neighbours when the park closed down in September 1979.

Later plans for its development as a leisure centre, as a golf course, and as a residential park of 149 houses all foundered and in 1993 it was bought by Norwegian shipping magnate, Andreas Ugland, and became a private house again.

Steam trains and natural gas

THE arrival of the railway was the making of modern Heathfield. The site selected by engineers in 1881 for the new station designed by T H Myers was in the parish of Waldron, half way between Old Heathfield and Cross in Hand. They were not to know that they had placed it on top of a deposit of natural gas.

The supply was discovered accidentally when the London, Brighton and South Coast Railway Company was boring for the water required in quantity for steam trains. The borehole had reached a depth of 377ft without tapping any underground spring or artesian well – but the engineers did notice a strong smell of gas. One of them decided to test its source and strength by applying a light to the top of the borehole. The result was an immediate whoosh of flame which was only put out with the greatest difficulty.

✳ ✳ ✳

COINS MARK
GAS STRIKE

COINS *were struck in*
1902 to commemorate
the coronation of King
Edward VII and Queen
Alexandra and the
discovery of natural
gas at Heathfield.
The face of each coin
shows the crowned
heads, the reverse the
inscription: Heathfield
Sussex 1902 Natural
Gas first used for light
and power.

✳ ✳ ✳

Until the start of the Second World War this gas supply, of up to about 14 candle power, was used to fuel the lamps in the station. The pressure was a formidable 140lbs to the square inch so fish tail burners, rather than incandescent mantles had to be used. Today all that remains above ground of Heathfield's natural gas supply is a standpipe.

At the parish council's insistence the new station was known as Cross in Hand. No one quite knew what to call the settlement that grew up around it and along the road to Burwash, but people living there did not like the postal address of Station Road accorded to it by the Post Office at Eastbourne. Heathfield Tower was suggested, and accepted, and appeared as a postmark until the mid 1930s.

When the Cuckoo Line, the name by which the single track rail link between Eastbourne and Tunbridge Wells was affectionately known, was closed in 1955 nature soon overgrew what man and machines had abandoned. That is until 1976 when Wealden District Council and East Sussex County Council stepped in, bought the line and transformed the length between Polegate and Heathfield into an award winning country path for walkers, cyclists, and the disabled – and called it the Cuckoo Trail.

The tunnel that took the railway line at a depth of 160ft under the High Street from the Co-op supermarket car park through to Station Approach has now also been restored. The work was done of necessity for it was falling apart and the drains were flooding. Wealden District Council has landscaped the entrance on the south side and plans to incorporate the tunnel with the Cuckoo Trail 200 yards away to the south.

To the Crusades – from Cross in Hand

THERE is no written record to confirm the romantic tradition that *Cruce Manus*, Cross in Hand, was where Crusader knights assembled with their esquires and men-at-arms on their way to the coast to take ship to the Holy Land. There is not much visual evidence of age in the locality either although the much altered Cross in Hand Hotel dates from around 1600 and displays a hand holding a quartered standard.

It has a tiny church, St Bartholomews, almost hidden from sight in trees on the right hand side of the road to Eastbourne – and what was the last working commercial windmill in Sussex. The white post mill, believed to be the largest in county with a post 2ft 6ins square, was brought from Mount Ephraim at Framfield in 1855 by miller William Kenward and stands on a bank on the north side of the Cross in Hand to

A mill on the move - with the aid of rollers and eighty six oxen.

* * *

THE SHOW
GOES ON

Only twice in the past fifty-two years has the Heathfield Agricultural Show not been held. The ending of the basic petrol ration stopped it in 1948 and an outbreak of foot and mouth disease caused the cancellation of the 1952 show.

Today the average attendance tops the 20,000 mark

* * *

Lewes turnpike, now the B2102, about half a mile from its junction with the A267. Some 100 yards from it is the round house of Cross in Hand's old mill, which ceased working in 1903.

The new mill was first sited on the opposite side of the road about a quarter of a mile further south. However, its presence there did not please art collector Louis Huth, the owner of Possingworth Park. He had spent £60,000 on the neo-Gothic mansion and the park that surrounded it so he could entertain his London friends in privacy. A windmill clacking away on the skyline was not what he wanted so it had to be moved.

With the aid of rollers and a team of oxen the mill was shifted to its present site in 1868 and continued to grind barley, oats and maize as feeds until 1969 when its stock broke while it was working.

Louis Huth died in 1904 and his nephew Frederick Huth, a governor of the Bank of England, inherited Possingworth. In the 1930s it was a luxury hotel; in the 1950s an Augustinian seminary and since 1964 the Sisters of Grace and Compassion, a Benedictine order of nuns, run it as a care home for the homeless, elderly and frail.

The first Heathfield Agricultural Show, now the largest one-day event of its kind in the south east, was at Cross in Hand on April 27 1946. It was run by the Heathfield branch of the National Farmers Union and raised £200 for the Sussex Hospitals Thanksgiving Appeal Fund. By the 1960s the show had become an annual event at Little Tottingworth Park, Broad Oak, on the last Saturday in May or first in June.

HURST GREEN

Location: Four miles east of Burwash at the
junction the A265 and A21.
Population: 1,417.
Station: Etchingham, one and a quarter miles to
the southwest.

WHEN Sussex was preparing its defences against the threat of invasion from Napoleon's forces this lookout platform, known as the Stage, was built for the field barracks set up on the top of Silver Hill, a mile to the south of Hurst Green. Horace Walpole inspected it in 1752 and described the view as 'a whole horizon of the richest blue prospect you ever saw'. The lookout was taken down in the 1930s but the land it stood on, now known as Stage Field, was given to the people of Hurst Green in 1949 by Colonel R T Hornblower of Etchingham as a memorial of the Battle of Britain.

The road that climbs over Silver Hill was one of the first gated turnpike roads in Sussex. The gates would not be lifted by the attendant pikeman – hence turnpike – until the traveller had paid the fee due for the maintenance of the road. This could be fivepence a score for a drove of calves, pigs, sheep or lambs; sixpence for a waggon with wheels of less than six inches in breath drawn by two horses, mules or beasts of draught and as much as two shillings for any four wheeled conveyance drawn by seven or eight draught animals.

In the early years of the reign of George III a public statute was passed for 'repairing, widening and keeping in repair the road leading from the Turnpike Road on Hurst Green in the County of Sussex (now the A21), through Etchingham and Burwash, to the extent of the parish of Burwash, in the said County. . .' That road is now the A265. The arrival of the railways took much of the wheeled traffic away from the roads

※ ※ ※

PLEASE STOP
THE CLOCK

*The courthouse clock
was erected by public
subscription as a
memorial to George
Burrow Gregory of
Boarzell, a member of
the Bench and a village
benefactor.
His granddaugher,
Chrissie Gregory,
released the pendulum
at the opening ceremony
in October 1892 – and
it started to strike the
hours on a bell
weighing two
hundredweight.
The sound not only
disturbed the nights'
sleep of the neighbours
but of the whole
village so it was
stopped – by public
request.*

※ ※ ※

and the Turnpike Trusts were wound up and their road responsibilities taken over from 1889 by the newly formed county councils.

The Hurst Green tollhouse was demolished in 1892 and a new court house, plus a police station and a lock-up, built on the site by East Sussex County Council at a cost of £1,680 for the Burwash Petty Sessional Division. Courts had been held at the Rose and Crown at Burwash until 1839 when a move was made to the Royal George at Hurst Green. There is a note in the Salehurst Vestry minutes of June 21 of that year to remind the members of the Burwash Bench of this change of venue.

From 1893 the magistrates were at Hurst Green's

new courthouse on the last Wednesday of the month at 11am to dispense justice to those summonsed to appear before them; deal with licensing applications and the occasional committal hearing. The courthouse was closed in 1973 and the premises, which still bear the county coat of arms, were sold and converted to offices.

Royal rescuer is honoured

THE royal coat of arms above the door of the Royal George is there for a reason. Queen Victoria stopped at the inn in 1841 to invest Mr Peckham Micklethwaite of Iridge Place, Hurst Green, with a baronetcy. It was her personal thank you for his gallant action four years previously when she was being driven in a landau along the St Leonards sea front and one of the horses became entangled in the traces and fell, dragging the other horse down with it. Princess Victoria, as she then was, described what happened in her journal:

> 'Two gentlemen very civilly came and held the horse's head down while we all got out as fast as possible. I called for poor dear little Dashy [her King Charles spaniel] who was in the rumble; Wood (our footman) took him down and I ran with him in my arms calling Mamma to follow. They then cut the traces, the horse still struggling violently. The other horse, which had been quite quiet, being frightened by the other's kicking. . . ran after us and we instantly ran behind a low stone wall. . . We ought to be grateful to Almightly God for His merciful providence in thus preserving us, for it was a very narrow escape. The names of the two gentlemen who held the horse's head are Rev Mr Gould and Mr Peckham Micklethwaite. The latter I am sorry to say was hurt, but not very materially. . .'

The royal arms on the Royal George were cast at the Hurst Green foundry. This was started in 1704 and continued as an engineering shop and foundry until 1972 when it was bought by Harper and Eede and the entire works – cupola, furnace, foundry, fitting and turning shop, pattern loft and smithy – was dismantled and re-erected at the Chalk Pits Museum at Amberley.

Bernherst, a manor house on the London Road opposite the Royal George has been the home of the Packenham family since 1821. First to

✳ ✳ ✳

MRS KNOX
GUARDS
IRIDGE

*The Knoxes, who
bought Iridge Place in
1933, were not so
kindly disposed to the
village as were the
Packenhams of
Bernhurst.
Mrs William Knox
quickly called a halt to
the school parties held
there by the Drewetts.
When she wanted the
gutters of the house
cleaned she would
lower a boy out of an
attic window on a rope
to do the job and when
an attempt was made
to requisition Iridge at
the start of the Second
World War she locked
the main gates and met
the military with a rifle
and several large
wolfhounds.*

✳ ✳ ✳

arrive was Miss Lucretia with her niece, Catherine Weekes, and they were joined by a nineteen year old French count, Pierre de Trazylle. He had shown the Duke of York an escape route from Valenciennes and the advancing army of Napoleon and in consequence needed to flee France. Admiral John Pakenham, who was on the Duke's staff, suggested his sister's place in Sussex as a safe house and there, until he died in 1857 at the age of eighty-three, the count stayed with 'Mrs Lucretia', as this maiden lady with her 'adopt-ed' extended family was affectionately known in the village.

Diplomat Sir Francis Packenham considerably enlarged Bernhurst in the early 1900s but it was probably his widow, Lady Caroline Packenham, an enthusiastic gardener, who had the Suffolk style 'wavy wall' built round the grounds to protect the plants and trees. It seems that walls that follow a ser-pentine rather than straight path round a property offer better wind resistance.

Lady Caroline, like Mrs Lucretia, was a good friend to the village. She gave the land in Station Road on which the village hall is built; performed the opening ceremony in 1927; and continued the school children's Christmas parties formerly held at Iridge Place until her death, at the age of ninety-six, in 1938.

Bernhurst is now the home of her nephew, the pre-sent Earl of Longford, and his Countess. Today, at the age of ninety-one, he regularly walks down to Robertsbridge, has tea with a friend, and is driven home.

MAYFIELD

Location: Eight miles north of Heathfield, now bypassed by the A267.
Population: 1,615.
Station: Wadhurst four miles to the north east.
Car park: Off the High Street, entrance opposite the gatehouse.

THERE are places in Sussex where time has stood still – and Mayfield is one of them. It still gives the impression of importance it had from the tenth century, when Dunstan was the first of a long line of medieval Archbishops of Canterbury to make it their official residence, to the Dissolution of the Monasteries in the reign of Henry VIII.

According to his biographer, the monk Eadmer, Dunstan, who was canonised in 1102, did much more for Mayfield than that. He built a wooden church there and, finding it incorrectly orientated, corrected the alignment by applying his shoulder to one corner and giving it a good push. He also caused a spring of water to issue from the ground by striking it with his staff so providing the palace with a water supply.

The saint had a legendary encounter with the devil and came off best. While he was working at his forge – for he was a skilled worker in metals and an architect of many fine cathedrals – the devil appeared before him in the guise of a beautiful woman. But Dunstan spotted a cloven hoof beneath her skirts and grabbed the apparition by the nose with a hot pair of pincers. The devil leaped into the air with him and came to earth three miles away by what is today called Dunstan's bridge at Mark Cross. There the saint released his hold and the devil bounded off to cool his nose in the springs at Tunbridge Wells which, in consequence, have been sulphurously mineral rich ever since.

Both Dunstan and the devil are on the village sign which won the £500 second prize in a national competition run by the *Daily Mail* in the 1920s.

MAYFIELD

* * *

ROYAL VISITS
COST MONEY

The palace was in the hands of Sir Thomas Gresham, builder of the Royal Exchange, when Queen Elizabeth I made her first progress through the county in 1573.
Entertaining royalty was an expensive undertaking in Elizabethan England. Sir Thomas Gresham spent £7,500 on the furnishing of the royal bedchamber, over the chimney piece of which is carved the Gresham crest of a grasshopper and the date 1571, the year the queen formally opened the Royal Exchange.

* * *

The sign was designed by Geoffrey Webb of East Grinstead and the girls with their garlands of flowers represent as a Maid's Field the Maghefeld of *The Anglo-Saxon Chronicles.*

By the fourteenth century Mayfield Palace had been extended by successive archbishops into one of the most impressive edifices in the land. King Edward I enjoyed its comforts on three occasions and in 1332 bishops and church dignitaries attended the provincial synod held there to rationalise the dates of church festivals and saints' days. It escaped the fire of 1389 which destroyed so much of medieval Mayfield and also survived the trauma of the Reformation and Dissolution of the Monasteries intact – Archbishop Thomas Cranmer simply handed it over to the Crown from which it passed to a succession of noble families.

The palace's decline began when Thomas May, considered by Dr Johnson to be 'the best Latin poet in England', inherited it and manor of Mayfield from his father, but with no money to keep it up. Thomas studied at Gray's Inn but possibly because of a speech impediment chose to earn a living from literature rather than the law.

Tom May died accidentally in 1650 – he suffocated himself by tying the strings of his nightcap to tightly – and was buried in Westminster Abbey. His body was unceremoniously disinterred at the Restoration and thrown onto a refuse pit because he had been a supporter of the Commonwealth. His epitaph, by Andrew Marvell, sums up his end quite neatly:

'As one put drunk into a packet boat
Tom Day was hurried hence and did not know't'.

The Archbishop's Palace, now occupied by the Convent of the Holy Child.

The palace's structural deterioration accelerated in the eighteenth century when it belonged to the Baker family. The roof was stripped off the 70ft by 40ft great hall built by Archbishop Simon Islip *c* 1350, leaving it open to the weather, and the materials used to build other houses in the village.

Victoria picnics at the palace

BY 1833, when fourteen year old Princess Victoria and her mother, the Duchess of York, were given lunch there by Lord and Lady De La Warr, it was a beautiful ruin. The royal party arrived dusty and dishevelled, having ridden over from Tunbridge Wells on the new turnpike road because the Earl of Abergavenny had refused them permission to ride through Eridge Park. He had made a rule that no visitors to Tunbridge Wells should have access to his grounds and he stuck to it. Lunch in the palace ruins was a cold collation provided by Mrs Homewood, the farmer's wife who acted as a resident caretaker.

✳ ✳ ✳

DUCHESS FUNDS A COLLEGE

Another school that owes it existence to the Duchess of Leeds and the design of its buildings to Pugin is Mayfield College in Little Trodgers Lane. It was intended for orphaned boys, as was the convent school for orphaned girls, and was handed over to the Xaverian Brothers in 1865.

However, when the generous Duchess died there were not the funds available for that purpose and both schools had to become fee-paying.

The college is now an independent Catholic boarding and day school for boys aged eleven to eighteen years.

✳ ✳ ✳

Thirty years later there was another picnic at the palace – one that saved it for posterity. Mother Cornelia Connolly, the American founder of the Society of the Holy Child Jesus, arrived with some of the girls from her school at St Leonards-on-Sea on an educational visit. She immediately became aware of its potential as a convent. It was quiet and secluded for the novices and for the older sisters and the park could be farmed profitably. But the bishop did not agree and refused to make funds available for the project. Which is where another American Roman Catholic, the widowed Duchess of Leeds, stepped in. She bought the palace and gave it to the Society of the Holy Child Jesus, on condition that it was restored and a school for orphan girls set up there.

E W Pugin, architect of the House of Commons, was commissioned to do the work and the nuns, who at first had to live in the old farm buildings, went out and about and begged for the £100,000 that was needed. They raised it all in nine years. On September 17 1872 the school's first intake of eight girls, the youngest aged two, arrived. Today St Leonards-Mayfield School has 500 pupils, two thirds of them boarders, and has been in the top 200 in the examination league tables every year since they were started.

Master of all trades

THE Free School, which was set up in the partitioned off south west corner of St Dunstan's church at a cost of £480 and entirely maintained by the people of Mayfield for its first 100 years, had a problem with its first headmaster. In 1749 parishioners advertised in the *Lewes Journal* for a member of the Church of England stipulating 'that he be of meek and humble behaviour; that he have good governance of himself and passions; that he has a genius for teaching; that he write a good hand and understand Arithmetic'.

They got former exciseman William Gale and paid him the meagre sum of £16 a year which he augmented by surveying, map making, selling books and stationery and carving inscriptions on gravestones. By 1758 his concentration on his commercial interests, and a fondness for the bottle, prompted the school managers to accuse him of neglecting the education of his twenty or so pupils, but it was not until 1771 that he was finally given a quarter's notice. The post was then advertised at the same salary 'with a very good dwelling house.'

Gale fought back at once with a series of letters to the *Lewes Journal* complaining about the poor state of the dwelling house, its water supply, the surrounding fences, 'the room in which the school is kept' and his treatment by the managers. He said he would start a school in another part of the town where he would teach:

> Writing in all its useful hands
> Arithmetic in its different branches
> Mensuration of every kind and the
> Italian Method of Accompts.

He died in 1773, before he could do so, and was buried at Framfield, carried there by twenty poor men from Mayfield who each received five shillings plus twenty-four shillings between them for expenses on the road.

The school in which Gale taught did not get purpose-built premises until 1815. They were on the site of the present school on the corner of Fletching Road and were extended in 1873 to make room for infants' classes and rebuilt in 1914. From September 1950, the year it celebrated its bi-centenary, it became a junior school only – the seniors having to travel to Heathfield. Today the 146 pupils of Mayfield primary school still have to use the old outside lavatories that date from the 1914 rebuild, although the first phase of an improvement scheme has recently provided them with a new hall and kitchen and there are more extensions in the pipeline

The sacred and the secular

✳ ✳ ✳

FIEND LEAVES FOOTPRINTS

When the stone church that replaced Dunstan's wooden one was being built, the devil undid at night whatever building work had been done during the day.
For years, so legend says, his footprints could be seen in the quarry near Old Mill Farm where he would spend the daylight hours obstructing the workmen who were cutting the stone.

✳ ✳ ✳

ST DUNSTAN'S church, almost completely hidden behind the buildings on the north side of the High Street, suffered from the usual devilish interference in its construction. It was partly destroyed by fire in 1389, severely damaged in the storm of 1621 and had its shingled spire struck by lightning in 1905. The latest catastrophe was in 1995 when a fire in the Lady Chapel damaged the organ. A fine new organ has been installed but it covers the squint which can now only be seen from the chancel.

All that remains of the thirteenth century stone church, which replaced Dunstan's wooden one, is the base of the tower with its heavy buttresses. On the exterior ironstone are burn marks which give an idea of the severity of the fire which was foretold, according to Thomas of Walsingham, by a young man of Ely to whom St Etheldreda appeared and predicted that there would be 'so great a heat as to melt the lead of churches'. The fifteenth century rebuild was in the Perpendicular style and gave the the church its two storey battlemented south porch. At daybreak on the first Sunday in May the church choir sings Easter carols from the roof of the porch.

In April/May of every other year since 1970, when Mayfield Festival of Music and Arts was founded by the vicar, the late Donald Carter, and Kenneth Pont, director of music at the convent and church, to raise funds to build a church hall, there have been classical concerts at St Dunstan's. Among the internationally known conductors and soloists who have appeared there are David Willcocks, John Ogden, Evelyn Glennie, Jean Pascal Tortellier, Vittoria de los

St Dunstan's church showing the two storey battlemented south porch

Angeles and, on the lighter side, jazz musicians Humphrey Lyttleton, Ronnie Scott and Kenny Ball. The church hall has not been built but twenty eight years later the festival continues to fulfill its other prime objective – that of providing the highest quality of music and art for the benefit of the community.

A cross indicating a church or chapel and the name St Mary in the Fields appear on present day large scale maps of Mayfield above a cul-de-sac off South Street. It was there until 1975, in wooden framed verandahed bungalows built from materials salvaged from First World War army camps at Newhaven by a local builder, that an Anglo Catholic order of nuns ran first a shelter for disadvantaged children and then an old people's home. The bungalows and the belfried chapel are now in private occupation.

The Sussex flint and stone Roman Catholic Church of St Thomas of Canterbury in Station Road looks medieval but is, in fact, modern.

Middle House, home of the Baker family of ironmasters for more than 140 years, has been an hotel since 1926.

Before it was completed in 1957 services had been held in the gatehouse of the convent.

A number of the historic houses in the High Street were either owned, occupied, built and/or altered by members of the Baker family of iron founders who bought the palace and manor of Mayfield in 1617. They had a strange family tradition that their funeral services had to be held at midnight – and gave St Dunstan's church the two handsome brass candelabra above the nave to provide the necessary illumination. The excessively Elizabethan black and white timbered Middle House, built in 1575 – according to the date carved on the bargeboards – was acquired by the Bakers in 1669 and they stayed there until 1841.

In 1926, when the old Star Inn burnt down, its license was transferred to the Middle House and for a time after the last war band leader Jack Payne and his wife Peggy Cochrane were the licensees and there were some merry impromptu concerts after last orders had been called. Now it is a luxurious eight bedroom hotel as well as an old world inn with magnificent floor-to-ceiling carved oak panelling in its restaurant.

The Bakers' next acquisition was Alywins, a mullion windowed stone house, screened from the High Street by a high stone wall, and now part of the convent school. It belonged to another family of ironmasters, the Aynscombes, from the time of Henry VI and then to John Fuller of Brightling, father of 'Mad Jack', who sold it to the Reverend Peter Baker, vicar of the Mayfield, in 1728. It was extended with materials removed by Michael Baker from the old palace, which he called Upper House and, as he already had Middle House, Aylwins became Lower House.

Michael was the keenest builder of all the Bakers. He used stone from the ruins to build Stone House, now St Joseph's, the guest house of the convent, and to block in the arched entrance to the palace and convert the fifteenth century gatehouse into a dwelling.

Walk into almost any shop in the High Street and you will find indications of the sixteenth century origins of the buildings they occupy. There is an inglenook fireplace in the hairdresser's and customers can look out through Tudor windows on to the churchyard of St Dunstan's. A few doors away, adjoining London House, the flowers, pine furniture and gifts of The Bazaar, Rose and Willow are displayed in heavily beamed rooms and alcoves beneath which are spacious cellars and a splendid example of a medieval undercroft. Ask nicely and you can have a look at it.

Villains and VIPs

NO town or village in the High Weald was without its smugglers. The Mayfield Gang, headed by Gabriel Tompkin, a bricklayer from Tunbridge Wells, set up its headquarters in Charity Cottages in Fletching Street and proceeded to move contraband around the county quite happily for several years. When, in 1721, the gang was finally broken up its leader turned King's Evidence and walked from the court a free man.

His next trick was to persuade the Customs service to accept him as a riding officer, which it did, presumably on the 'set a thief to catch a thief' principle. However his former smuggler friends made life so difficult for him that he left the law and the area and tried his hand at highway robbery. That was the last trick of Gabriel Tomkins, alias Young Gibb, alias Kitt Jervis, alias Christopher Wood, alias Unkle, alias Rawlins. He was found guilty at Bedford Assizes in 1750 of robbing the Chester mail and on March 23 of that year he was hanged and his body left in chains by the roadside at Hockley, where he had held up the coach.

Wild Irishman George Hawkes who lived at Downford, a large house off Fir Toll Road, had the town dancing in the streets when a ball he gave at the Star in the 1880s broke up. The county had arrived by the coachloads from Eridge and elsewhere but left in embarrassment when their host and one of his fellow

✳ ✳ ✳

MARTYRS'
MEMORIAL

There is a memorial in front of what is now Colkins Mill Evangelical Free Church in Station Road to the four men of Mayfield who, in 1556, were burnt at the stake for their Protestant beliefs.
It was put up in 1950 when the building, erected by Wesleyan Methodists a century before, was a Congregational Church.
In 1972, when the Congregationalists and Presbyterians amalgamated it became a United Reformed Church.

✳ ✳ ✳

countrymen starting fighting on the ballroom floor. George, finding his guests gone, called for more wine, made it up with his erstwhile enemy and moved the party outside to dance until dawn with the celebrity-watchers in the street. He even persuaded the bellringers, who had joined in the jollity, to greet the new day with chimes from the church. Their somewhat pickled peal woke the vicar, the Reverend Henry Kirby, and he was not pleased, when he appeared on the scene, to have two drunken Irishman trying to embrace him while his parishioners continued to party.

It was not for a party, but to avoid the police, that militant suffragette leader Emmeline Pankhurst came to Mayfield in 1913. She did not stay in the village with her late husband's relations, who had lived there for centuries, but spent two months in hiding in the cellars of Woodside, the home of Dr Hedges, whose wife was one of her keenest supporters.

Comedian and broadcaster Richard Murdoch, co-star with Kenneth Horne of the long running radio show Much-Binding-in-the-Marsh, had his out-of-London home in Knowle Road in the 1950s. He would always help out when any charity event wanted a personality to open the show, judge the jam or present the cups.

Lord Godber, one-time head of Shell Oil, took Mayfield as his title when he received his peerage. His country home was Cranesden, a sixteenth century farmhouse much altered by the sculptor John Woolmer when he lived there in the 1870s. It is reached from a lane off West Street. Nearby is West Wood where General Sir John Bagot Glubb lived in retirement after his dismissal from the Jordan army at the time of the Suez crisis.

Miscreants at Mark Cross

THE miscreants of Mayfield – and Crowborough, Rotherfield and Wadhurst – appeared before magistrates of the Frant Petty Sessional Division at Mark Cross from around 1880 until the little wood panelled courtroom there was closed in the 1980s. The village was at the junction of the old Mayfield-Frant and Rotherfield-Wadhurst turnpike roads and, as at

* * *

LAST TRAIN

Mayfield once had a railway. It arrived in 1880, linking the main line west of Eridge with the branch line to Hailsham.

The last train steamed away in 1965 and the station and Station Hotel are now houses and flats and the new bypass carries the road and its traffic along the line of the old track.

* * *

Hurst Green, its toll house was converted to a police station and a courthouse added. On the second Tuesday of every month the place would be packed with horse drawn and, later, horse powered vehicles while justice was dispensed by the Bench.

Mark Cross had a school before it had a church. It was built in 1851 by Henry Dixon of Frankham as Frankham Church of England School and twenty-two years later a vestry was added, internal alterations made and it was consecrated as St Mark's church. The dispossessed pupils were moved to new classrooms next door and the present Church of England primary school came into being.

Mark Cross has had a number of residents whose names are internationaly known. Film star Susannah Yorke and her husband, Michael Wells, lived at Frankham; Sir Adrian Boult, principal conductor of the London Symphony Orchestra, and Lady Boult, had their country home in a house converted from the annexe of Tower Mill; and Dr Sophia Jex-Blake, who pioneered the cause of women in medicine, retired in 1899 and spent the last twelve years of her life at a house originally called Sandyden with her friend, Dr Margaret Todd, who was also a novelist. Her most successful book was *Windydene* and this was the name given to Sandyden House during her occupancy.

ROBERTSBRIDGE

Location: On the A21 trunk road six miles north
of Battle, but now bypassed to the east.
Population: 1,155.
Station: In Station Road.
Car park:Also in Station Road.

THE design on the village sign by the clock tower settles the argument about the original name of this settlement. Some say it was Rotherbridge, because it has a bridge over the Rother. However, the sign is based on the seal of Robertsbridge Abbey, founded in 1176 by Robert de Sancto Martino, and the P and R shown each side of the abbey church spire are from the Latin *de Ponti Roberti* – the Bridge of Robert or Robert's Bridge.

Today there is a business-like bustle about this large main road village with its old and new houses climbing south up the hill towards Hastings and, since the 1860s, west past its railway station on the road to Brightling and Burwash. Robertsbridge, in spite of its size, is not a parish and has no church of its own. It is in the large ecclesiastical parish of St Mary's, Salehurst, a village on the north bank of the Rother with a present population of fifty-five.

In earlier days the social centre and gossip exchange of the area was the seventeenth century George Hotel in the High Street, where the London coaches stopped to change horses. It was from the George, in 1902, that Hilaire Belloc started out on the journey through Sussex he describes in his travel fantasy, *The Four Men*.

Some years earlier the legendary Dr W G Grace had stayed there on his way to play cricket at Hastings. Perhaps it was on that occasion that he bought the bat with which he scored his 100th century from Levi Nicholls, a carpenter and keen cricketer who, in the 1870s, had started making bats for his friends in his shop in the High Street.

ROBERTSBRIDGE

Wealden timber framed houses in the High Street and, below, the
Seven Stars Inn

100

Gray Nicholls Sports Goods Manufacturers, a subsidy of Gray's International, is still making cricket bats in Robertsbridge, now in modern factory premises in Station Road. In the firm's archives, among commendations from such great players as Ranjitsinghi, Hirst and Bowley, is a letter from W G Grace, written in 1895. In it he says:

> 'I used one of your bats at Hastings in 1894 and scored 133 runs. I may mention it was perfectly new. I kept it until this year and have scored over 2,000 runs with it. I used it when I made my 100th century and scored 1,000 runs in May with it. So I think I may call it my record bat. '

One of the oldest and most architecturally interesting buildings in the High Street is the medieval timber framed Seven Stars with its outside stone steps. This inn, which has been much altered over the years, was a private house until the early eighteenth century and originally belonged to the Cistercian Abbey of Robertsbridge, the remains of which are close to the river at the end of Fair Lane.

In the past twelve years or so Gerard and Melissa Williamson, who live in the Robertsbridge Abbey farmhouse, have spent much time and money restoring the remains of the abbey within its walls and outbuildings. Sadly most of the monastic buildings were removed, stone by stone, by earlier generations of Robertsbridge residents who regarded the site as their private quarry and helped themselves to whatever they needed in the way of buildings materials.

Historians argue over who founded St Mary's Abbey, Robertsbridge in 1176. Was it Robert St Martin, named in the Chronicle of the church of Rochester, or his kinsmen, Alured de St Martin, named in a charter granted by Richard I in 1198? Richard certainly had cause to be grateful to the Abbot of Robertsbridge for he, together with the Abbot of nearby Boxley Abbey, had secured the king's release from imprisonment in Bavaria four years previously.

This success appears to have given the monks of Robertsbridge a taste for litigation. In 1250 they embarked on what turned out to be an eight year long legal dispute, which ended in a compromise, over the ownership of 100 acres of land in Burwash. They were more successful in 1284

ALL THE FUN
OF A FAIR

A charter for a fair on September 14, the Feast of the Exaltation of the Holy Cross, was granted to the Abbot of Robertsbridge in 1254. It was held in a field off Fair Lane – hence the road's old name. It is now East Street. A cattle market was held on the site until the 1950s when it was transferred to Battle.

* * *

when judgement was given in their favour in two cases relating to abbey lands at Salehurst and Ewhurst. Two years later they won again when a claim for damages for the wrongful detention of James Prenlyn's cattle failed.

The monks were also kept busy by a steady stream of royal visitors, among them Henry III (twice), Edward I (once en route from Winchelsea to Westminster) and Edward II who had two oxen roasted whole for him and his entourage and a cheese brought down from Norfolk.

By the fifteenth century it appears that it was not law but disorder that occupied the fraternity – but the state forgave them. In a retrospective type royal pardon the abbot was acquitted not only of 'any infringement of statute law of which an upright man might be guilty' but also of 'all kinds of robberies, murders, rapes of women, rebellions, insurrections, felonies and conspiracies' providing they were committed before September 2 1432.

The monks were in trouble again some sixty years later. Abbot John Godewine, three brothers and five yeomen of Robertsbridge were charged with disturbing the peace by entering a house in North Bridge Street 'with swords, staves, knives and other arms' and 'there and then digging and obstructing the course of the rivulet called the Lyme.'

When the abbey was given by the Crown, after the Dissolution, to Sir William Sydney – grandfather of the 'thy need is greater than mine' Sir Philip – it housed, from around 1540, a furnace and forge planned by a parson. The vicar of Salehurst and steward of the Sydney household, Sir John Horrocke created, according to Ernest Straker, author of

Wealden Iron, 'a remarkable piece of engineering for such an early date.' Bar iron was produced at first but the manufacture of steel started at Robertsbridge in the mid sixteenth century and continued at the abbey ironworks until 1801.

In 1971, a good four centuries after the Cistercians left, the only Hutterian community in Britain moved into Darvell, a former TB sanatorium on the Brightling Road. Here 250 men, women and children live to a pattern established by the first community of Anabaptists set up in Moravia in 1528. They are pacifists; they refuse to vote or swear oaths; and they hold all property in common.

To get an income they make toys and equipment for disabled people and keep in touch with events in the outside world by radio – they decided against television. Members of the Darvell Bruderhof are instantly recognisable by their style of dress which is reminiscent of the early settlers in America's bible belt. The men are all bearded and wear tunic jackets over gingham shirts and braces. The women are in calf length dresses and their polka dot scarves are tied beneath the chin.

Robertsbridge was a busy rail junction until 1954 when the branch line to Tenterden was closed. It was operated by the Rother Valley Light Railway which, when the line was extended to Headcorn, became the Kent and East Sussex Railway. Hundreds of East Enders, bound for their annual working holiday in the hopfields, would arrive from London on the South Eastern Railway and pack into the Ostrich by the station for a drink before catching a branch line train for Bodiam or Northiam.

Members of the Kent and East Sussex Railway Society have restored a steam train rail service between Northiam and Tenterden but the old rail bridge over the Rother is not strong enough for trains to cross it to Robertsbridge.

The Church of St Denys, Rotherfield.

ROTHERFIELD

Location: On the B2100 three miles east of
Crowborough
Population: 3,096
Station: Crowborough and Jarvis Brook

O NE of the oldest townships in the
High Weald is right next door to
the newest. In 792AD, 500 years before Crowborough was even a
name on a deed, the Saxon duke, Berhtwald, gave 'all that estate of mine
called Ridrefeld. . .with all its appurtenances, lands, fields, pastures,
plains, woods and streams. . . to the holy martyrs of God, Dionysius,
Rusticus and Eleutherius, to have control and hold for ever. . . '

The gift to the three saints – St Denys, the first Bishop of Paris, his
priest and sub-deacon – was in return for a miracle cure performed in
their name when Berhtwald prostrated himself to their memory in the
Abbey of St Denys in France. He had travelled there, suffering, he says,
'from a sickness no doctors could cure,' and in a very few days, 'I, the sick
man . . . was completely healed.

> 'Wherefore I vowed an offering to God and those saints, and I brought with
> me the protection I had gained from their sacred relics . . . and built a church
> on my estate in the property called Ridrefeld which had been bequeathed to
> me by my ancestors.'

Which is how Rotherfield came to have a church dedicated to the
patron saint of France and an alien Benedictine priory – alien because it
was set up by monks sent from a foreign abbey. There were some 130
other such priories in the country, seven of them in Sussex – at Arundel,
Hove, Beeding, Sompting, Steyning, Wilmington, Lyminster – but they
had all been dissolved by the end of the fourteenth century.

The Benedictines left Rotherfield very much earlier. The church and
lands the St Denys Abbey had been given 'to hold for ever' were handed

*** ***

ST MICHAEL
MURAL

Still visible on the left side of the chancel arch is a winged St Michael weighing the souls of the departed.

*** ***

by a charter of William II to the Bishop of Rochester in 1089.

Where the priory was is not know. Several sites have been suggested – opposite the church, in Court Meadow, in Chant Lane – but no stones or artefacts have yet been unearthed to provide positive identification. The present church is part Norman, part Early English with later additions. The tall, shingled spire, visible from miles around, came crashing down in the 1987 hurricane and has since been rebuilt.

During repairs to pillars in the south aisle in 1893 a fifteenth century Doom painting was discovered and when the rest of the church was examined there were signs of wall paintings all over it. They are thought to date from the thirteenth century and were covered with egg white to preserve their colours. This has not preserved their medieval brilliance of the reds and golds but even faded they are fascinating.

Another find was the bowl of the church's ancient font. It was discovered by a former rector, Canon Frederick Goodwyn, sunk into the ground at Horsegrove, a 176 acre estate belonging to George Wray, a man not good with money. By 1893 he had mortgaged the property so heavily that he could not keep up the repayments. The mortgagees foreclosed and sold the estate to recoup the £14,000 owing to them. They also sold the font to the rector for five shillings and it is back in the church. The tall font cover behind it is made up of oak panels carved with the date 1533, the arms of George Nevill, then lord of the manor and the heads of men and animals.

Canon Goodwyn was also indirectly responsible for the church acquiring the beautifully-carved fifteenth century pulpit from the Archbishop of York's private chapel at Bishopsthorpe. His wife was the daughter of the Most Reverend William Thompson, Archbishop of York from 1863 to 1891, and she had it brought to Rotherfield and erected at St Denys as a memorial to her father.

There is no authentication of the wide-held belief that the Eastern Rother rises in the cellars of Rotherhurst – a mile to the south on the road to Five Ashes – but certainly maps show it rising in the grounds of the house.

In 1853 Rotherhurst was leased by actress Mary Anne Clarke – a person with a past, in the Victorian sense of the word. She had been the mistress of Frederick, Duke of York, who was forced to resign as commander-in-chief when she was accused of accepting bribes for obtaining commissions in the army for her friends. After the death of her royal protector and a series of libel actions she moved to Paris, making only occasional visits to England.

The original font, recovered by Canon Goodwyn, and beside it the carved font cover.

Her presence at Rotherhurst accounts for how Punch artist and author of *Trilby*, George Palmella Lewis Busson du Maurier, father of actor/manager Sir Gerald and grandfather of the novelist Daphne du Maurier, came to be baptised in Rotherfield church. Mrs Clarke was his grandmother and her daughter and son-in-law had come over from Paris to visit her.

In the early eighteenth century it seemed that almost every other house in the High Street was a hostelry. Opposite the Catt was the Bull; opposite the Kings Arms was the Three Guns, so called because it chimneys are shaped liked banded cannon; and the George was by the

❋ ❋ ❋

STREET MARKET

On the May and October fair days householders boarded up their windows in case they were broken by the horns of passing cattle.

For the fairs were held in the main street and gipsies watered their horses in Johnsons Pond by the church.

After the First World War the fairs were replaced for a time by stock auctions in Court Meadow.

❋ ❋ ❋

churchyard. Today only the George, the Cats Inn, and the King's Arms, pictured above, on the corner of the High Street and New Road, are still dispensing food, drink and hospitality. In the 1950s the licensee of the latter was the Maurice Tate who, during his career in first class cricket, took 2,211 wickets for Sussex.

In one of Rotherfield's inns, which one is not specified, a Prosecuting Society was formed in 1791 for the purpose of bringing to justice the four man gang which had been terrorising the neighbourhood. In March that year four masked men knocked down farmer John Bridger's housekeeper when she answered the door, tied her up and stole all the pieces of silver and cash they could lay their hands on. The four had been identified and the society offered a reward of £15 for the arrest of each robber. Two were caught, convicted and sentenced to death but later reprieved and instead transported for fourteen years.

TICEHURST

Location: Two and a half miles east of Wadhurst
on the B2099.
Population: 3,118.
Car park: North side of the High Street, entrance
from Pickforde Lane.
Station: At Stonegate, two and a quarter miles to
the south west, or at Wadhurst.

THE great forest of Andredesweald, the Silva Anderida of Roman Britain, was without any significant human occupation in this area until the eleventh century. Hence Ticehurst or Tysehurst, the wood on the Tees (a tributary of the Medway) was yet another manor that did not make the Domesday survey. It did, however, make history in May 1264 when 315 hostages were beheaded there. It also made history on May 17 1940 when the first bombs to fall on Britain in the Second World War killed a pony at Pickforde and destroyed a chicken house and forty hens at Landscape Farm.

In 1264 Henry III was on his way through the Weald to enlist the support of the Cinque Ports in his dispute with the barons, led by Simon de Montfort, when his cook, Thomas, was killed 'by a certain countryman' as he rode ahead of the armed column as it crossed the Kent border. Henry's royal revenge for this assault on a member of his entourage is described in the *Chronicles of Battel Abbey:*

> 'He caused many of the people of the country assembled above Flimwell whither they had been ordered by Lord John de la Haye, an adherent of the barons, to be surrounded like so many innocent lambs in the fold, and beheaded'.

On that May morning, 'in the presence of the king in the parish of St Mary at Ticehurst' the hostages had their heads cut off. The royal party then moved on to Robertsbridge where Henry was welcomed and feasted by the hospitable Cistercians.

✻ ✻ ✻

LAUGHTER
IN CHURCH

Services at St Mary's were not always as seemly as they should be when Frank Chapman, an eighteen year old labourer, was in church.
He was fined five shillings, with sixteen shillings costs by magistrates at Hurst Green in May 10 1861 'for laughing and otherwise disturbing the peace of the congregation on several occasions during divine service at the parish church of Ticehurst'.
If he did not pay the fine the alternative was thirty days in the county gaol at Lewes.

✻ ✻ ✻

St Mary's church.

The Church of St Mary, newly built at the time of this medieval massacre, has a Doom stained class window depicting the Day of Judgement. Six people roast in a cauldron over a fire, watched from the edge of the flames by naked figures, and one wearing trousers. An angel with a drawn sword flies above and below a cart filled with the damned is moved along by ape-faced fiends.

During the nineteenth century restorations, when the Doom was removed from the east window to the north wall of the chancel, a 2ft 3ins wide slab was discovered by the communion rail at the side of the chancel. The three brasses on it show how the executor of Sir John Wybarne's widow complied with her instructions 'to buy a convenient stone and lay it upon my husband's grave and mine in the chancel of Tysehurst' without contravening Sir John's instructions to be buried near to his first wife, Edith. He obtained a massive brass of a knight in late fourteenth century armour to represent Sir John who died in 1490, and on the sides of it he fixed the much smaller brasses he had made depicting Sir John's two wives.

Above the church porch is a room with a window which was covered by a grating until later restoration gave it mullioned panes of glass. Like a similar porch room at St Dunstan's, Mayfield, it was used for a variety of purposes, including, occasionally, for the confinement of felons.

In the porch itself is a list of the 331 men and women from Ticehurst who fought in the First World War, the majority of them in C Company of the 5th (Cinque Ports) Battalion of the Royal Sussex Regiment, under the command of Captain George Courthope of Whiligh. May has been a sad month for Ticehurst throughout history and it was on May 9 1915 that most of the sixty two who never returned died when the Royal Sussex Regiment was cut to pieces on Aubers Ridge in the battle of Festubert. Eleven of them were on the staff of Cooper's Stores and to this day their names can be seen on a brass plaque fixed to the wall of the premises that faces the church.

A two room building in the

The pentice roof supported by cast iron columns outside Cooper's Stores – a Wealden way of prviding shelter for shoppers .

111

COACHES IN CONFLICT

Warren Coaches, a firm started in 1920 by Philip Warren with a Model T Ford lorry, still has its headquarters in the High Street. Between the wars there was much undercutting of fares and rivalry over routes as local coach operators fought for business. Warren Comfort Coaches ran a twice daily express service to London with single fare s at 4s 9d and returns 5s 9d. Competitors Autocar and Red-Car were taken over by Maidstone and District but Warren Coaches survived and today operates a luxury European travel service.

✳ ✳ ✳

churchyard housed the village school until a national school was built in 1846. Its three to twelve year old pupils had five weeks' hopping holiday every year, plus occasional days off if extra hop-picking help was needed.

It was not until 1600 that Ticehurst had grown enough for the lord of the manor, Thomas Pelham, to get permission for two annual fairs to be held there. From then on the expansion was rapid, thanks largely to hops and the Sussex iron industry. Brick and tile hung houses and cottages went up in Church Street and the High Street and, although their front elevations of the latter may have been altered over the years, the attention the seventeenth century builders paid to the chimneys they placed on their roofs is still evident.

Care for the rich – and poor

IN the 1760s, when the insane were often treated as criminals and locked away until they came to their senses, which few of them did, Samuel Newington, surgeon and apothecary of Ticehurst, was pioneering a more humane approach. He was the first of a family of doctors who believed that those with mental disorders would be more likely to recover if they were cared for in pleasant surroundings.

By the 1830s, when Ticehurst House was advertising accommodation for patients 'of a superior station in life' its surroundings were extremely pleasant. There were walks, plantations, a cricket pitch, croquet lawn, an archery range, a bowling green, a Chinese gallery, a museum, billiards rooms and other indoor amusements in its 200 acres as well as a handsome chapel.

Ticehurst House Hospital

In 1914, the year in which Dr Alexander Newington was killed when his car overturned while passing a lorry on the road to Wadhurst, Ticehurst House became a private company but carried on much as before with Dr Herbert Newington as medical superintendent. After the Second World War, however, there were great changes. The farms and all the land that went with them were sold, the ornamental buildings in the gardens demolished. In 1973 the institution was sold to Allied Medical and in 1986 to Nestor Medical Services after which it became independent as the result of a management buy out. Ticehurst House Hospital, one of the country's foremost psychological institutions, is now a public company listed on the Stock Exchange.

The village not only offered a centre of care for the rich. The poor of eight adjoining parishes were looked after in Ticehurst workhouse, built at Flimwell in 1836 and later called Furze House. While the Newingtons' patients had the best that money could buy at the west end of the village the inmates of the Union workhouse at the east end had to make do with the little the contributing parishes could afford. So it was an iron church

✳ ✳ ✳

WELL BEFORE BEWL

Before Bewl an earlier source of water was the village well.
Fund raising for it started with a bazaar in 1885 and the well – in front of the Duke of York Inn – was in use three years later.
Today there is a seat instead of the well-head, winding handle and bucket under the tiled roof built to mark Queen Victoria's golden jubilee..

✳ ✳ ✳

for the staff and inmates rather than a handsome chapel that the Bishop of Chichester dedicated on August 7 1876. These period pre-fabs, which needed little in the way of foundations, were quick and cheap to construct and are to be found in many of the villages of the Weald doing duty as a House of God for various denominations.

Ticehurst lost some land but gained a share of a magnificent stretch of water in 1972/3 when a tributary of the Medway, the River Bewl, was dammed and the valley to the north of the village flooded to create the 770 acre Bewl Reservoir. Dunster Mill House would have been totally submerged had not its owner, Hubert Beale, successfully petitioned Parliament for its preservation. The Southern Water Authority paid for the fifteenth century house to be dismantled brick by brick and rebuilt above the waterline, some 500 yards away. The machinery of Dunster watermill that had survived the fire of 1951, which totally destroyed its timber framed and weatherboarded superstructure, was also saved from submersion and re-sited with the house.

WADHURST

Location: On the B2099, nine miles south west
of Tunbridge Wells.
Population: 4,499.
Station: In Station Road. London 58 mins
Car parks: In Washwell Lane and off
Greyhound Lane, behind the Greyhound Inn.

IRON industry riches have left this ridge-top town a fine architectural legacy. It is surrounded by great houses; its church is almost paved with iron grave slabs; it has a castle, a Commemoration Hall and a station designed by William Tress on one of the highest railway summits in the south.

The village sign, erected to mark the 700th anniversary of the charter of Henry III for the holding of a weekly market and a fair on June 29, the feast of St Peter and St Paul, is on the site of the old turnpike gate on the western approach to the town. The charter, which was obtained from the king by Archbishop Boniface in 1253 and conferred on Wadhurst the status of town, has survived and is now in the safe keeping of the parish council. Today neither market nor fair is held there. The last cattle market was on August 23 1982 and the market hall was blown down in the October 1987 hurricane. The annual three day fair, which was held on Cheesman's Field, faded away between the wars.

Wadhurst, like so many other settlements in the High Weald, is not mentioned in the Domesday survey. Its name, from the Old English *Wadan hyrst*, Wada's wooded hill, first appears in the twelfth century when 'Simon de Srimonte and his wife gave to the Abbey of Battel all his land in the parish of Wadehurst'. It was then, like Ticehurst, a typical forest clearance community relying on pannage, charcoal burning and woodland related occupations for its survival. Oaks in the park at Whiligh, a manor held by the de Courthopes from 1255, were felled at

✳ ✳ ✳

BEARING
ARMS

Massive stone bears on the gate pillars of Snape Lodge hold shields emblazoned with the Barham coat of arms.

the request of King Richard II to provide timber to roof the great hall he was having built at Westminster in 1395. Oak from Whiligh was used in the sixteenth century to build the ships that fought against the Spanish Armada and in modern times, when Westminster Hall's roof was in need of repair, Sir John Courthope, who just happened to be a national authority on forestry management and joint founder of the Forestry Commission, had plenty of the necessary on his estate on the Wadhurst/Ticehurst border. Sir John, who was raised to the peerage in 1948, was MP for Rye from almost forty years.

The iron ore in the Wadhurst clay was smelted in furnaces fuelled by wood from the forest and forged into wheel rims, horse shoes, swords and ploughshares and, as more land was cleared, more crops were grown, more stock raised, more homes were built. This quiet, rural idyll of craftsmanship and crop cultivation changed in the mid 1500s. The iron industry, once the first cannon was cast, was put on a wartime footing to face the threat from Spain and, with valuable contracts to be filled, the sound of hammer on anvil rang out day and night along the forest ridges.

The Barham family of Wadhurst was one of the first to make a fortune out of iron – and to lose it. From the late 1600s they built or re-built fine houses on the estates they acquired, which included Shoesmiths to the north; Snape and the Scrag Oak furnace to the south; Great Butts to the east; and Coushopley to the west of the town – and rose from being yeomen to gentlemen in a generation.

However, through misfortune, mismanagement and the collapse of the iron industry they were back working with their hands again by the 1780s when Nicholas Barham died a pauper, as did his son, a carpenter known as 'Old Buckram', in 1791.

They were wealthy and at Wadhurst again by 1885. In that year George Barham, who started the milk business that became the Express Dairy Company, bought the Snape estate and, as his ancestors had done before him, built an imposing mansion there. He had memorial inscriptions to such illustrious members of his family as 'John Barham, High Sheriff of Sussex, 1699; the Reverend R H Barham author of *The Ingoldsby Legends*' and his late wife 'Lady Barham, Mayoress of Hampstead, 1836-1906' inscribed on the sandstone outcrops in the woods behind his house at Snape and gave the area the name of The Sanctuary. Sir George – he was knighted in 1904 – was a friend of the Prince of Wales, afterwards King Edward VII.

Another personal friend of the prince, Christobel de Murietta, who came from a noble Spanish banking family, had acquired the neighbouring Hightown estate, owned by the Maunser family of ironfounders from the sixteenth century. He changed the name to Wadhurst Hall and set about making it a fit place in which to entertain a future king of England. With his brother, Adriano, he enlarged the house, adding a private chapel, a riding school, a ballroom and all the mod cons of the day. A tea house was built by the Tide Brook so the prince, accompanied on occasions, so it is said, by his friend of the musical theatre, Lily Langtry, could have some privacy, and a vast lake was made in the park so he could indulge in his favourite sport of duck shooting. However, giving British royalty a good time proved too much for the noble Spaniards. By 1899 they were bankrupt and had to sell both their Burwash and Wadhurst estates.

Wadhurst Hall was snapped up by Julius Charles Drew who had opened a grocery shop in Liverpool in 1878 and retired, a rich man, ten years later. He remained a shareholder in the Home and Colonial Stores, the company he had founded, but devoted the rest of his days, from the age of thirty-three, to leading the life of a country gentleman. He added a final 'e' to his name by deed poll, having established to his own satisfaction that he was descended from the Drewes of Devonshire and from

Single storeyed and with a great use of colour – John Outram's post-modernist Wadhurst Park.

Wadhurst Castle as it is today.

a Norman noble called Dru or Drogo who had crossed the Channel with the Conqueror. Until 1928, when he moved to the castle in Devonshire which he had commissioned Edwin Lutyens, the fashionable architect of the day, to build for him, he lived at Wadhurst with his wife and daughters and was attended by seventeen indoors servants and a number of gardeners and gamekeepers.

The estate was renamed Wadhurst Park by the MacLeans who occupied it until the 1939-=45 war, when it was requisitioned by the army. The house made fit for king was demolished after the war and at one time there were plans to develop the 800 or so acres as a theme park. So intense was the local opposition to this suggestion that WASP, the Wadhurst Area Society for Protection and Preservation, was set up to oppose it.

In 1976 a post-modern single storey building designed by John Outram was built for the present owner and the estate is now a deer park. It has, as well as the native fallow deer, herds of Sika from Manchuria, white spotted Axis deer from India, and the rare Pere David deer discovered by French missionary Armand David in the Imperial Hunting Park in Peking. When the Wadhurst herds are culled the venison is sold to game dealers or London restaurants and the antlers to the United States and Germany where knife handles, buttons and other articles are made from them.

Another purchaser with an urge to re-build, and to change his name, was James-Louis Lucadou. He obtained a royal licence to use his grandmother's maiden name of West and in 1818 he demolished Maplehurst, a fourteenth century farmhouse approached by a long drive opposite the road to Sparrow's Green, and replaced it with a square, castellated stone house with a turret at each corner. It was inherited by his natural son, Henry Talbot who, seven years later, exchanged it for a house in France owned by Aylmer Haly.

Henry fancied himself as an historian and produced *The Red Book of Wadhurst*, six hand-written and unpunctuated pages of tortured prose. The author wrote it, he explained, 'to bring to his own knowledge some little acquaintance with a Place which will probably be his place of future residence the entering upon which inquiry is a curiosity not only

✳ ✳ ✳

TREES NOW
SHED LEAVES
ON THE LINE

*In the days of steam
the trees in the woods
south of Wadhurst
through which the
trains passed were
often set on fire by
hot cinders from the
coal-fired engine.
Since electrification
the trees have had their
revenge and 'leaves on
the line ' have on
occasions disrupted
autumn and winter
timetables.*

✳ ✳ ✳

to be pardoned but if omitted would betray a mind insensible to everything around it.'

And he goes on: 'The situation is very elevated commanding extensive views. . . but these beauties are counterbalanced by the uncivilised state of the inhabitants and the high level of taxation. . .' However, he does include the occasional snippet of historical information such as: 'One Watson who lived at Maplesden kept his carriage and regularly attended divine service drawn in carriage by eight bullocks.'

It was Aylmer Hayly who changed the name of the house he had acquired by exchange to Wadhurst Castle. Later owners enlarged it to make it look even more worthy of that name. The 'castle' was badly damaged by fire in the 1930s but it has been re-built.

Trouble with the tunnels

ALL did not go well when the railway came to Wadhurst in 1851. The lowest tender from an untried contractor was accepted and the work, when completed, was not to the required standard. The tunnels were unsafe – bricks dropped from the roof of one of them – and they had to be re-lined and so reduced in width. Which was all very well until the 1920s when wider trains came along and could not be used on the line. Specially built stock had to be used until the 1950s when straight sided six coach diesel electric trains were introduced and stayed in service until the 1980s when the line was electrified àt a cost of £20 million and the tunnels widened.

The station, a mile and a quarter to the east of Wadhurst, was one of several designed by William Tress for the SECR, affectionately known as Slow,

Wadhurst station.

Easy and Comfortable Railway. From the start it offered a motor-rail service of a sort so the rich were able to take their own carriages with them on long journeys. The conveyances were loaded on to a flatbed and swung in a ninety degree arc on a turntable and pushed across the main line on traversing rails to another turntable at the end of the opposite platform. From there the flatbeds were moved to a siding to await the arrival of the train to which they would be coupled.

That £1,000 prize fight

THE government decree which made bare fisted prizefights illegal prompted devotees of the sport to stage a series of tip and run contests in the Home Counties. The promoters chose secluded sites close to a railway giving easy access from London and on county boundaries so they could, if dispersed, say, by the police of Sussex, escape into Surrey or Kent to avoid pursuit.

The site chosen for the £1,000 prize fight between American champion

John Heenan and English champion Tom King was at Turners Green. At 6.15 on a fine December morning in 1863 a special thirty coach train left London Bridge packed with promoters, fighters, bookies, punters and spectators.

It pulled up short of Wadhurst station at 6.15am and the ring was set up, so says the report in *The Times*, 'in the midst of a valley surrounded by high meadows'.

The fight lasted for forty minutes during which, says *The Times*: 'sundry, flat-nosed men, whom no one would think of trusting out of handcuffs, swagger about and loudly offer 100 to 5 on the American . . . and the spectators call out in hungry accent for closer fighting and more blood'.

At the end of the twenty-fourth round Heenan was virtually insensible and was withdrawn reluctantly by his friends. King, the victor, could hardly stand, and all round the ring there was blood in the grass until the next rains came.

The High Street

ALTHOUGH Wadhurst has town status there is a friendly village feel about its High Street which is lined on either side with a variety of shops and services. There is also the White Hart, next to which is the Commemoration Hall and Institute – the hall was built by the British Legion as a First World War memorial – which houses the parish council offices and a branch of the East Sussex County Library. Further east, on the same side, is the Greyhound, a posting inn dating back to the sixteenth century and one of the notorious Hawkhurst Gang's safe houses.

❋ ❋ ❋

FIGHTERS HAD
POLICE ESCORT

The police helped rather than hindered the fight that broke the law. They turned out in force in London to escort the contestants to the train but took no further action once it had left the station. As a result there was no police presence at Wadhurst and few local people even knew the prizefight had taken place.

❋ ❋ ❋

The parade of shops on the left side of the High Street was built after the aircraft crash which destroyed the Queen's Head Hotel.

England all rounder Maurice Tate, previously at the King's Arms at Rotherfield, was the licensee of the Greyhound for a number of years until his sudden death in 1956. He is buried in Wadhurst churchyard.

In that year tragedy also struck the Queen's Head Hotel, the centre of village social life for many years. On January 20 a Royal Air Force plane on a training exercise crashed into the hotel, destroying it and the adjoining International Stores and some cottages in Washwell Lane. Two of the occupants of the cottages – seventy four year old Thomas Stamp and his housekeeper Emily Reed – were killed and so was the pilot, Flying Officer Alan Stoates, a Wadhurst man, and his navigator, Alastair Patterson from Ayrshire. The inquest verdict was that the plane was flying too low.

Away from the hurly burly of the High Street, which achieves traffic calming by the absence of double yellow lines and the presence of many parked cars, is the parish church of St Peter and St Paul which has a 128ft high spire and thirty-three iron grave slabs, two of which are in the churchyard.

The spire has been struck by lightning six times since it has been on the Norman tower of the church. On it is a large gilded pennon vane

* * *

OLD IRON – AND SOME NEW

It is not all old iron in Wadhurst church. This glass and wrought iron screen of a flight of swallows and leaping lambs was designed by Duncan Wilson in 1957 and the cast iron cross and candlesticks on the altar were made ten years later.

* * *

fretted with the date 1699 and the letters TC and RC – perhaps the initials of the churchwardens in office when the spire was repaired or re-shingled.

The ironmasters of Wadhurst chose to have their last resting places marked by slabs cast in their family foundries. The work was often done by apprentices and moveable blocks would have been used for the six shields beneath three stars and the date 1617/WB on William Barham's grave slab.

There are six different shields, all placed askew, on the grave slab for 'AB 1634' and five additional sets of initials and dates from 1717 to 1789 have been inscribed on it as later Barhams were buried. The family's coat of arms appears for the first time, quite simply executed, on the slab of David Barham of Snape who died in 1643. On the massive 7ft 9ins by 2ft 8ins slab of eighty year old William Barham, who died in 1701, the arms are handsomely embosssed in high relief.

Until Joseph Newington, who started a grocery business in Wadhurst in 1810, built the St John the Baptist's church at Tidebrook in 1856, the people of that hamlet had a long walk to church, either at Wadhurst or to St Dunstan's at Mayfield. Hans Wagner, one of the crew of the German bomber that crashed in the grounds of nearby Wadhurst Hall in 1940, is buried in its churchyard.

Almost opposite the church is the drive leading to Tidebrook Manor. This Tudor period farmhouse with Queen Anne additions was originally called Reed's until another business man seeking seclusion and a place in the country bought it in the nineteenth century. Glasgow publisher Alfred Blackie was the first of a number of people associated with literature and the arts who later owned the house.

For eleven years from 1950 composer Michael Tippett lived there with his mother and when they moved to the Cotswolds it was bought by stage and screen star Rex Harrison, but much to the disappointment of his fans in the area he never moved in. From 1969 it belonged to television newscaster Reginald Bosanquet and he sold it to the present owners.

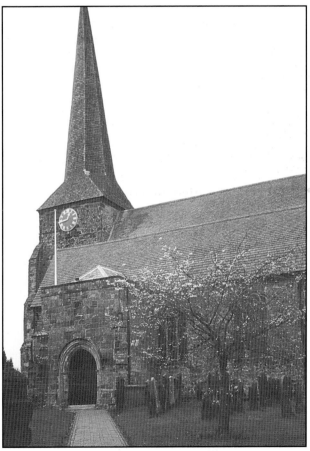

St Margaret's church, Wadhurst

BIBLIOGRAPHY

A Compendious History of Sussex by Mark Anthony Lower 1870
A Short History of the Parish of Salehurst by Leonard J Hodson 1914
Burghersh by Clement Woodbine Parrish 1949
Burwash and the Sussex Weald by James Goodwin. Courier Printing and Publishing Co 1959
Buxted the Beautiful by K H McDermott 1929
East Sussex Villages by Rupert Taylor. Countryside Books 1988
Hadlow Down, Sussex. Its Origins and History by Frederick T Barratt 1970
History, Antiquities and Topography of Sussex by T W Horsfield 1835
Hurst Green Recollections compiled by Ann Jenner. Hurst Green Historical Society
Illustrated Guide to Crowborough by Boys Firman. Hansard Publishing Union 1890
Mayfield by R C G Foster. 1964
Sussex Folk and Sussex Ways by J C Egerton. Methuen 1924
The Eastern Rother by Robert H Goodsall. Constable 1961
The South East from AD1000 by Peter Brandon and Brian Short. Longman 1990
Ticehurst, Stonegate and Flimwell by Francis Drewe. Phillimore 1991
Victoria History of the Counties of England – Sussex. University of London Institute of Historical Research 1973
Wadhurst, Town of the Weald by Alan Savidge and Oliver Mason. Meresborough Books 1988

Sussex Archeological Collections
Sussex County Magazine 1927-1956

Newspapers
Kent and Sussex Courier
Sussex Express and County Herald
Sussex Weekly Advertiser

Kelly's Directories of Sussex 1874-1938

INDEX